SEISMIC REHABILITATION AND RETROFITTING

JIMMY GUPTA
GUNJAN

First Published in April 2023

ISBN: 978-93-5704-925-2

BLUEROSE PUBLISHERS

www.BlueRoseONE.com

info@bluerosepublishers.com

+91 8882 898 898

Cover Design:

Muskan Sachdeva

Typographic Design:

Rohit

Distributed by: BlueRose, Amazon, Flipkart

Preface

Beam-Column joints are critical regions in reinforced concrete or RCC structures which are most vulnerable or sensitive to seismic forces because shear failure of joints is one of the main causes of collapse of many moment-resisting reinforced concrete (RC) buildings in recent earthquake activities. Evidence from recent seismic action indicates that deficient beam-column joints can jeopardize the integrity of the entire structure and shear failure of brittle joint also significantly reduces the overall ductility of structures but now days, a variety of techniques have been developed to strengthen beam-column joints. These techniques include the use of steel or concrete jacketing and use of fibre-reinforced polymer (FRP) as externally bonded reinforcement in critical regions of RC elements. This study contributes to investigate the effectiveness of strengthening beam-column joints using synthetic fibres sheet. In this book, Aramid fiber reinforced polymer which is a type of synthetic fibres, was used for strengthening and rehabilitant of beam-column joints with the help of epoxy reason. Araldite GY 257 and Hardener HY 840 were used as epoxy to make better bond between concrete surface and FRP sheet. FRP materials have a number of advantages over steel and concrete that make them an ideal material in strengthening deficient beam-column joints. Hence strengthening and rehabilitant beam-column joint by FRP is imperative to save the structure and its inhabitants in case of earthquake forces. Even the number of institutions where the concept of retrofitting and rehabilitation is being taught in civil/structural engineering and architecture, either as compulsory or optional has been increasing enormously. There are hardly a few books on this subject written in simple language and covering the theories and applications together.

The study on the subject matter is step by step and systematic and an attempt has been made to explain briefly the general principles of the subject. The unique feature of this book is that it is written completely in the Indian context. It is selfexplanatory and an easy read for the beginners in the subject.

Jimmy Gupta

Gunjan

Acknowledgements

First of all, we would like to thank God for keeping us in good health throughout the project development and for giving us strength for completing the project. A work spanning over several months entails the help and cooperation of many people directly or indirectly. Writing a book is harder than we thought and more rewarding than we could have ever imagined, even having an idea and turning it into a book is as hard as it sounds. We are obliged to the contributors whose knowledge and experience helped us to make this hard task possible and we especially want to thank the individuals that helped make this happen as without the experiences and support from our peers and team, this book would not exist.

Last but not the least we are deeply obliged to our family members for their encouragement and undefined moral support, and also thankful to the Blue Rose publishers for translating the seeds of our idea into a concrete reality. To the valuable readers, any unworthy mistakes are entirely ours and we own them in full measures.

LIST OF FIGURES

LIST OF TABLES

CONTENTS

Introduction

1.1 GENERAL

Concrete roles in construction is known to everyone, several structures were built using concrete such as multi-stories buildings, Flyovers, bridges etc., Concrete is nothing but a combination of binding material, fine aggregates and course aggregates with proper percentage of water and when reinforcement uses in it, called Reinforced concrete (RCC) which is a versatile material, popularly used worldwide in many structures. How-ever, its performance during seismic or earthquakes activity has created lot of questions in the mind. Seismic activity may cause reinforced cement concrete structures to collapse, loss of many leaving lives and staggering economic losses too. Many of the structures in our country are not able to resist seismic action even moderate. Under earthquake activity, it is imperative for RCC structures to have lateral resistance capacity against brittle break-down. Non-earthquake resistant buildings which designed by using non-seismic code of practice are vulnerable to seismic excitations so to make them seismic resistant, buildings should be reconstruct or retrofit. But reconstructing and demolishing RC buildings are too expensive where retrofitting the limited fraction of structural components and building can offer a workable solution for ensuring the safety of structure and people where retrofit is the strengthen and modifications to existing commercial or non-commercial structures that may improve energy efficiency or reduce energy demand. In addition, retrofits are often used as opportune time to install or inaugurate distributed generation to any structure. But Seismic retrofitting is modification of existing buildings to make them more resistant against earthquake or seismic action, ground motion etc.

In the analysis of reinforced concrete moment resisting frames the joints are generally assumed as rigid. In Indian practice, the joint is usually neglected for specific design with attention being restricted to provision of sufficient anchorage for beam longitudinal reinforcement. This may be acceptable when the frame is not subjected to earthquake loads. There have been many catastrophic failures reported in the past earthquakes, in particular with Turkey and Taiwan earthquakes occurred in 1999, which have been attributed to beam-column joints. The poor design practice of beam column joints is compounded by the high demand imposed by the adjoining flexural members (beams and columns) in the event of mobilizing their inelastic capacities to dissipate seismic energy. Unsafe design and detailing within the joint region jeopardizes the entire structure, even if other structural members conform to the design requirements. Since past three decades extensive research has been carried out on studying the behaviour of joints under seismic conditions through experimental and analytical studies. Various international codes of practices have been undergoing periodic revisions to incorporate the research findings into practice. The paper is aimed at making designers aware of the theoretical background on the design of beam column joints highlighting important parameters affecting seismic behaviour of joints.

1.2 STRUCTURAL BEHAVIOUR UNDER SEISMIC ACTIONS

Intolerable behaviour of structure and its components under earthquake or seismic action shown in figure 1.1 forced to think about dynamic integrity of structure and how can be improve it under dynamic or cyclic action of load. The philosophy of earthquake design relies on providing acceptable and sufficient ductility to the reinforced concrete structures so that structure can dissipate dynamic or seismic energy, where the ductility of any structure essentially comes from the member ductility of same structure wherein the latter is accomplished in the form of in-elastic rotations and in-elastic rotations or movement spread over definite regions of reinforced concrete members called as plastic hinges. The actual material attributes are beyond elastic range during in-elastic deformations and hence damages in these areas are accessible and obvious. The expected locations of plastic hinges are depends on structural damages which occur due to in-elastic actions involving large deformations. Hence, damages formed in beam regions, in the form of plastic hinges are accepted in seismic design, rather than formed in columns. Mechanism with beam yielding is predominance of strong-column weak-beam deportment where the demands of imposed in-elastic rotational can be accomplished reasonably well through appropriate detailing practice in traverse members like beams.

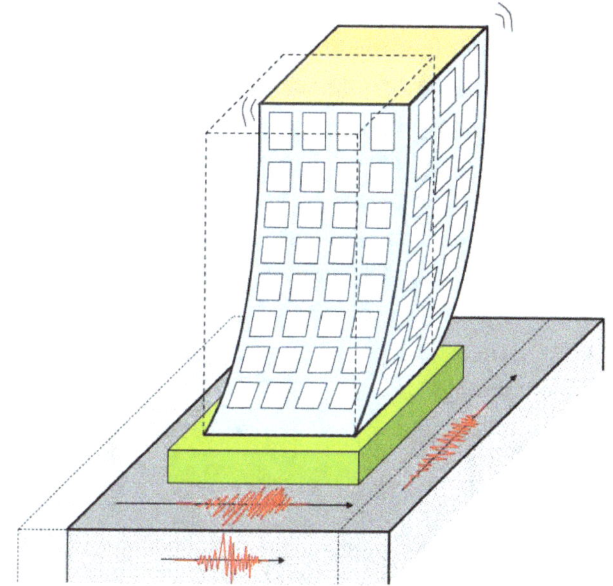

Fig. 1.1 Behaviour of Structure during Seismic Action

Therefore, it is possible in this mode of deportment, for the any structure to acquire the desired ductility and in-elastic response. But in other side, if plastic hinges are allowed to form in axial members like columns, the demands of in-elastic rotational imposed are too high which is very hard to be stayed with any thinkable or possible detailing and this mechanism is known as column yielding or storey mechanism.

One of the basic requirements of design is that the axial members or columns below and above the beam-column joint should have adequate flexural strength when the adjoining horizontal members or beams produce flexural over-strength on plastic hinges which formed on it, and the column to beam flexural strength ratio is a major parameter to making sure that possible plastic hinging occurs in beams rather than in columns.

1.3 BEAM-COLUMN JOINT

The Beam-Column Joint is the crucial as well as critical zone in a reinforced concrete moment resisting frame as shown in figure 1.2. It generally assumed as rigid, is subjected to large forces during seismic activity or severe ground shaking and its performance has a significant influence on the response of the building. The functional requirement of a joint, which is the zone of intersection of beams and columns, is to enable the adjoining members to develop and sustain their ultimate capacity. The joints should have adequate strength and stiffness to resist the internal forces induced by the framing members but lot of buildings are there in India which are non-earthquake or seismic resistant. This type of weak buildings creates large casualties of leaving lives during moderate or heavy natural ground shaking so, aramid fibre reinforced polymer (AFRP) sheet used here to overcome this major loss and to provide sufficient strength.

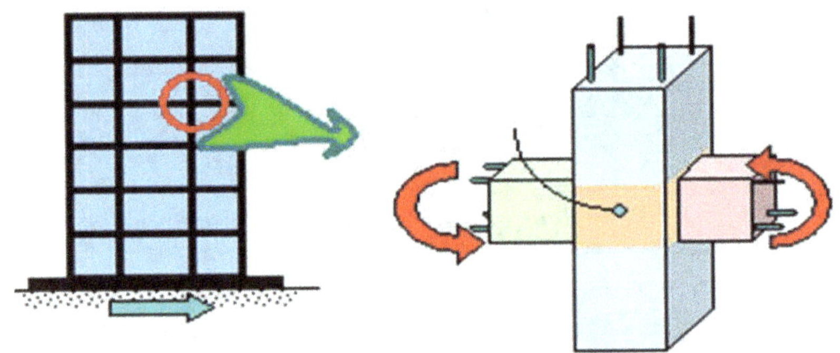

Fig. 1.2 Beam-Column Joint of Building

1.3.1 TYPES OF BEAM-COLUMN JOINTS

The beam-column joint is defined as the common portion of beam and column or in other words- portion of the axial member like column within the depth of the deepest beam that frames into the single column. Three different types of joints such as interior joint, exterior joint and corner joint, can be identified in a moment resisting frame as shown in figure 1.3.

When combination of four beams is attached into the vertical faces of a single column, that joint is known as an interior joint. When one horizontal member or beam into a vertical face of the axial member or column and two other beams frame from right angle directions into the joint, that joint is known as an exterior joint and when a beam frame attached with two adjacent vertical faces of a column, that joint is known as a corner joint.

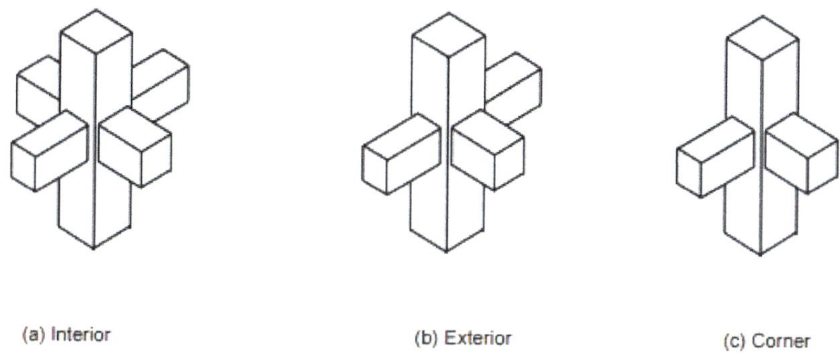

Fig. 1.3 Different Types of Beam-column Joint

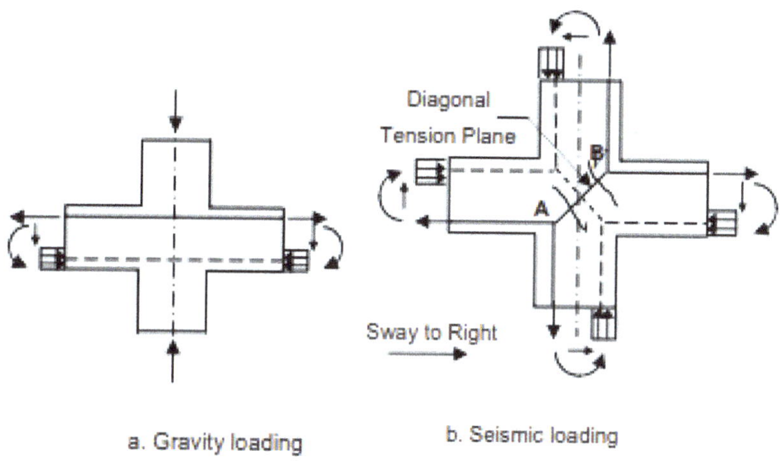

Fig. 1.4 Action of Force on Different Interior Beam-column Joints

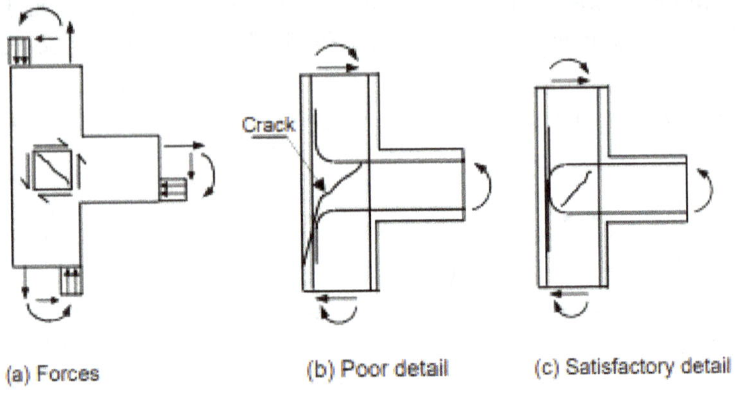

Fig. 1.5 Action of Force on Different Interior Beam-column Joints

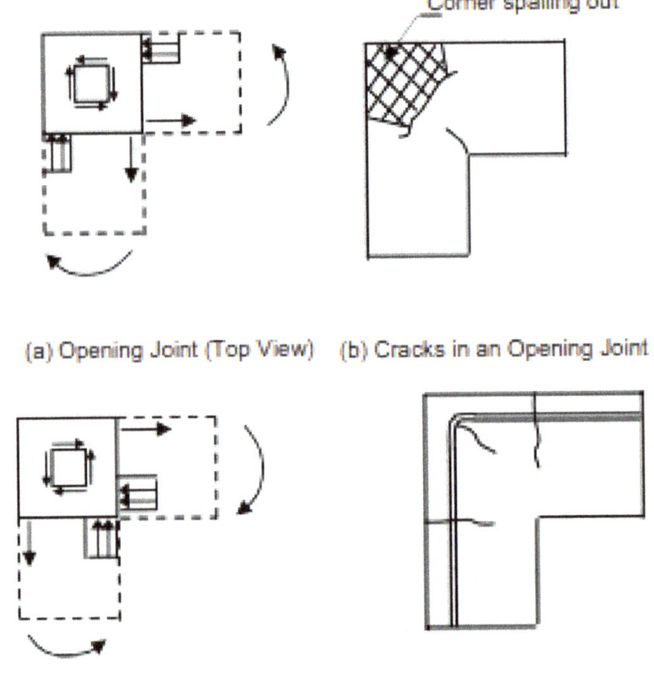

Fig. 1.6 Action of Force on Different Corner Beam-column Joints

1.3.2 FORCES ACTING ON A BEAM COLUMN JOINT

The pattern of forces acting on a joint depends upon the configuration of the joint and the type of loads acting on it. The effects of loads on the three types of joints are discussed with reference to stresses and the associated crack patterns developed in them. The forces on an interior joint subjected to gravity loading can be depicted as shown in figure 1.4(a). The tension and compression from the beam ends and axial loads from the columns can be transmitted directly through the joint. In the case of lateral (or seismic) loading, the equilibrating forces from beams and columns, as shown in figure 1.4(b) develop diagonal tensile and compressive stresses within the joint. Cracks develop perpendicular to the tension diagonal A-B in the joint and at the faces of the joint where the beams frame into the joint.

The compression struts are shown by dashed lines and tension ties are shown by solid lines. Concrete being weak in tension, transverse reinforcements are provided in such a way that they cross the plane of failure to resist the diagonal tensile forces. The forces acting on an exterior joint can be idealized as shown in figure 1.5. The shear force in the joint gives rise to diagonal cracks thus requiring reinforcement of the joint. The detailing patterns of longitudinal reinforcements significantly affect joint efficiency. Some of the detailing patterns for exterior joints are shown in figure 1.5(b) and figure 1.5(c). The bars bent away from the joint core (figure 1.5(b)) result in efficiencies of 25-40 % while those passing through and anchored in the joint core show 85- 100% efficiency. However, the stirrups have to be provided to confine the concrete core within the joint. The forces in a corner joint with a continuous column above the joint (figure 1.3c) can be understood in the same way as that in an exterior joint with respect to the considered direction of loading. Wall type corners form another category of joints wherein the applied moments tend to either close or open the corners. Such joints may also be referred as knee joints or L-joints. The stresses and cracks developed in such a joints are shown in figure 1.6. Opening corner joints tend to develop nascent cracks at the re-entrant corner and failure is marked by the formation of a diagonal tensile crack. The detailing of the longitudinal reinforcement significantly influences the behavior of such joints.

The forces developed in a closing joint are exactly opposite to those in an opening corner joint. The major crack is oriented along the corner diagonal. These joints show better efficiency than the opening joints. During seismic actions, the reversal of forces is likely and hence the corner joints have to be conservatively designed as opening joints with appropriate detailing. Failure of opening corner or knee joint is primarily due to the formation of diagonal tension crack across the joint with the outer part of the corner concrete separating from the rest of the specimen. Special and careful detailing is required to avoid failure of such joints so that the strength of adjacent members could be developed. The design and detailing schemes of these joints is beyond the scope of this paper and relevant information can be obtained elsewhere.

The stress resultants from the framing members are transferred into the joint through bond forces along the longitudinal reinforcement bars passing through the joint and through flexural compression forces acting on the joint face. The joints should have enough strength to resist the induced stresses and sufficient stiffness to control undue deformations. Large deformations of joints result in significant increase in the storey displacement.

Performance Criteria

The moment resisting frame is expected to obtain ductility and energy dissipating capacity from flexural yield mechanism at the plastic hinges. Beam-column joint behaviour is controlled by bond and shear failure mechanisms, which are weak sources for energy dissipation. The performance criteria for joints under seismic actions may be summarized as follows:

- The joint should have sufficient strength to enable the maximum capacities to be mobilized in the adjoining flexural members.

- The degradation of joints should be so limited such that the capacity of the column is not affected in carrying its design loads.

- The joint deformation should not result in increased storey drift.

1.3.3 JOINT MECHANISMS

In the strong column-weak beam design, beams are expected to form plastic hinges at their ends and develop flexural over strength beyond the design strength. The high internal forces developed at plastic hinges cause critical bond conditions in the longitudinal reinforcing bars passing through the joint and also impose high shear demand in the joint core. The joint behavior exhibits a complex interaction between bond and shear. The bond performance of the bars anchored in a joint affects the shear resisting mechanism to a significant extent.

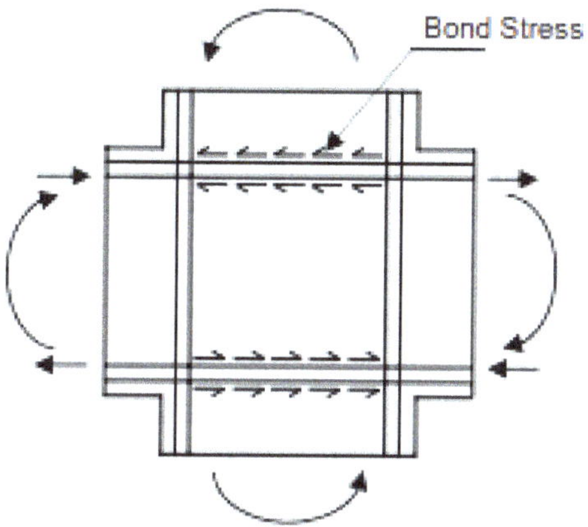

Fig. 1.7 Bond Stress in Interior Joints

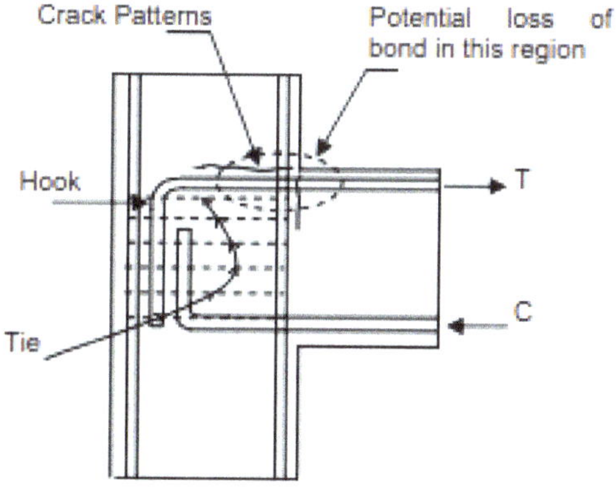

Fig. 1.8 Hook in an Exterior Joint

Bond requirements

The flexural forces from the beams and columns cause tension or compression forces in the longitudinal reinforcements passing through the joint. During plastic hinge formation, relatively large tensile forces are transferred through bond. When the longitudinal bars at the joint face are stressed beyond yield splitting cracks are initiated along the bar at the joint face which is referred to as 'yield penetration'. Adequate development length for the longitudinal bar is to be ensured within the joint taking yield penetration into consideration. Therefore, the bond requirement has a direct implication on the sizes of the beams and columns framing into the joint.

1. **Interior Joint:** In an interior joint, the force in a bar passing continuously through the joint changes from compression to tension. This causes a push-pull effect which imposes severe demand on bond strength and necessitates adequate development length within the joint. The development length has to satisfy the requirements for compression and for tension forces in the same bar. The distribution of bond along the longitudinal bars is shown in figure 1.7. Insufficient development length and the spread of splitting cracks into the joint core may result in slippage of bars in the joint.

    Slippage of bar occurs when the limiting bond stress is exceeded within the available development length. In the case of interior joints, the column depth is the available development length for the straight longitudinal bars passing through the joint. Hence, for a given limiting bond stress, the ratio of development length to the bar diameter becomes a constant value. Research has shown that when the development length is greater than 28 bar diameters little or no bond degradation was observed with respect to various shear stress levels in the joint. In other words, to avoid bond deterioration, the column depth should be around 28 times the diameter of the bar. This observation suggests the adoption of relatively smaller bar diameters so as to obtain with smaller depth of columns. For example, if 20 mm nominal bar size is to be used, the member depth to be provided is 560 mm.

2. **Exterior Joint:** In exterior joints the beam longitudinal reinforcement that frames into the column terminates within the joint core. After a few

cycles of inelastic loading, the bond deterioration initiated at the column face due to yield penetration and splitting cracks, progresses towards the joint core. Repeated loading will aggravate the situation and a complete loss of bond up to the beginning of the bent portion of the bar may take place. The longitudinal reinforcement bar, if terminating straight, will get pulled out due to progressive loss of bond. The pull out failure of the longitudinal bars of the beam results in complete loss of flexural strength. This kind of failure is unacceptable at any stage. Hence, proper anchorage of the beam longitudinal reinforcement bars in the joint core is of utmost importance.

The pull out failure of bars in exterior joints can be prevented by the provision of hooks or by some positive anchorage. Hooks, as shown in figure 1.8 are helpful in providing adequate anchorage when furnished with sufficient horizontal development length and a tail extension. Because of the likelihood of yield penetration into the joint core, the development length is to be considered effective from the critical section beyond the zone of yield penetration. Thus, the size of the member should accommodate the development length considering the possibility of yield penetration.

When the reinforcement is subjected to compression, the tail end of hooks is not generally helpful to cater to the requirements of development length in compression. However, the horizontal ties in the form of transverse reinforcement in the joint provide effective restraints against the hook when the beam bar is in compression.

3. **Corner Joint:** In a corner joint with column continuing above and in knee type joints, the bond requirements of longitudinal bars of beams will be similar to that in an exterior joint though there are no specific code requirements related to bond for knee joints. However, the performance of these joints is significantly influenced by shear diagonal cracks.

The bond deterioration along the beam reinforcement results in the following undesirable consequences:

- Beam deformation is increased prior to beam flexural yielding.
- Large beam end rotation associated with large crack opening accelerates concrete crushing at the face of the joint.
- Repair of bond deterioration is difficult.

1.3.4 REQUIRMENTS OF BEAM-COLUMN JOINTS

The essential requirements for the satisfactory performance of building during an earthquake can be summarized as follow:

- A joint should exhibit a service load performance equal to or higher than that of the members it joins. The failure should not occur within the joints.

- According to 'N Subramanian (Author of a Book: Design of Reinforced Concrete Structures), A joint should possess strength not less than the maximum demand corresponding to the development of the structural plastic hinge mechanism of the structure. This requirement will eliminate the need to repair a structure in an inaccessible region.

- In moderate earthquakes, the joint should behave elastically.

- The deformation of joints should not significantly increase the story drift or should remain within permissible limits.

- The joint configuration should ensure good access for placing and compacting concrete and ease of fabrication in the joint region.

- If deformation under the action of lateral forces is to be reliably quantified and subsequently controlled, designers must make a realistic estimate of the relevant property called stiffness. It is related to loads or effects ensuring structural deformations.

- If the concrete structure is to be protected against damage during a seismic event, inelastic deformation must be prevented during its dynamic response. This means that the structure must have sufficient strength to resist the internal actions that occur during the dynamic response. Therefore, based on the stiffness properties, the appropriate technique should be used to evaluate seismic-induced effects.

- Beam column joint is designed to minimize significant damage and to ensure the survival of buildings with moderate resistance with respect to lateral forces. Also, structures must be capable of sustaining a high proportion of their initial strength when a significant earthquake imposes large deformations.

The joint block area is relative to the member sizes, so it is essential to consider localized stress distribution within the joints. A simplified force system can be adopted in designing beam-to-column joints.

The required steel quantity is calculated on the assumption that steel reaches the design yield stress and the concrete its designed compressive stress. Where local bearing or bond failure is expected, the lower of the two capacities should be adopted based on experimental results. It is essential to prevent anchorage and bond failure within the joints through proper beam-column joint detailing and design practices, especially at the external joints.

The Design Procedure of Beam-Column Joints in Reinforced Concrete Structure Consists of the Following Basic Steps:

- Start from the preliminary size of members based on anchorage requirements for the chosen longitudinal bars.

- To get the desired beam yielding mechanism, ensure sufficient flexural strength of columns.

- Arrive at the design shear force for the joint by evaluating the flexural over strength of the adjacent beams and corresponding internal forces in columns that maintain equilibrium.

- Obtain effective joint shear area from the adjoining member dimensions.

- Ensure that the induced shear stress is less than the allowable stress limit. The allowable shear stress limit is expressed as a function of diagonal tensile strength or the compressive strength of concrete. If not satisfied, alter the associated member dimensions.

- Provide transverse reinforcements both as shear reinforcement and as confining reinforcement.

In most cases, the reinforced concrete joint is a rigid joint because of the monolithic nature of the material. However, it is the reinforcement detailing or the way in which reinforcement is placed offers the member rigidity or flexibility. Hence, beam and column joints are rigid or flexible depends upon the detailing.

Fig. 1.9 Failure of Structure due to Failure of Joint

1.3.5 EFFECTS DUE TO IMPROPER ANALYSIS OF JOINTS

Beam column joints are special in buildings, these are portions of columns familiar to beams at their intersections and are made of constituent materials that have limited strengths; hence, the joints have limited force carrying capacity. The joints are severely damaged when forces larger than these are applied during earthquakes. Repairing damaged joints is complex, so damage must be avoided; beam column joints must be designed and detailed to resist earthquake effects.

During an earthquake loading, joints in structures are inferior to most other types of joints. The failure of joints connecting columns and girders frequently occurs, causing the building to collapse as shown in figure 1.9. Joint failure results in a change of angle between the columns and beams, and the building starts titling progressively till it collapses.

1.3.6 FAILURES OF BEAM-COLUMN JOINT

Beam-Column joint is the crucial zone of any structure or in simple words it is a root of building if it fails, then the entire structure would be damage. There are two major failures of joint which are as follows:

SHEAR FAILURE: Shear failure of joints is one of the main causes of collapse of many moment-resisting reinforced concrete (RC) buildings in recent earthquake activities as shown in figure 1.10. Evidence from recent seismic action indicates that deficient beam-column joints can jeopardize the integrity of the entire structure and shear failure of brittle joint also significantly reduces the overall ductility of structures. The mechanism of shear failure in beam is introduced by shear sliding along a cracks or faults without shear reinforcement and yielding of stirrups in a beam. Shear in joints is taken to be transferred by both of compressive force in concrete strut born between bent up part and beam compressive zone and tensile force generating in this type of joint transverse reinforcement after cracks produces in concrete. Shear strength of joint is taken by yielding of joint reinforcement or compressive fracture of concrete strut.

Fig. 1.10 Failure due to shear action

ANCHORAGE FAILURE WITH HOOKED BAR: This is a major type of joint failure looks only in moderate and heavy intensity earthquake or seismic action as shown in figure 1.11. This happens always due to improper detailing of anchorage bars or mostly in singly reinforced beams where main reinforcement uses always in tension side.

There are three types of anchorage failure which are defined in Indian design guideline as follows;

a) **Side splitting failure**: This of failure looks only when concrete located adjacent side of bent portion is ruptured in split, when the cover thickness of concrete is not suitable or convenient.

b) **Local compressive fracture**: This of failure happens only when, due to bearing stress concrete is ruptured located inside of bent portion, when bent radius of reinforcement is not sufficiently immense.

c) **Raking-out failure**: When concrete composite located opposite of bent portion is kicked out or raked out as one body.

Every type of this failure is caused by immense compressive stress produced inside of bent portion. Some types of failures are able to abstain by means of reinforcement detailing or cover concrete such as Type-A and Type-B as discussed above.

Fig. 1.11 Failure due to Anchorage

1.4 REHABILITATION OF STRUCTURES

Rehabilitation of any structure or building means returning to a useful state by means of modification, repair and alteration. When structural stability, safety and occupant of any building are in danger then can say building is said to require rehabilitation as shown in figure 1.12 and 1.13, and the term rehabilitation falls in structural significance. Rehabilitation of structure is cheaper way to regain the original strength of structure and make the structure improvements instead of reconstructing and demolishing, and constructing a new building.

1.4.1 REHABILITATION AND REPAIR OF STRUCTURE

There is basic difference between the words "rehabilitation and repair". Any structure or part of structure is said to require rehabilitation, when safety and stability of any structure and also occupant of it, is in danger or critical where the word repair generally indicates petty and small repairs more or less cosmetic, that are not belonging from structural significance.

In simple words, rehabilitation means approach the trouble and difficulty by the recognising of main culprits responsible for deterioration, for decreasing in strength. But in repair, plaster is used and apply only that does not last long hence it leads leakage in pipe lines, terrace etc. which produces a major reason of corrosion of RCC structure's reinforcement so can say plastering is nothing but the waste of money and time only and the conclusion is came from this discussion is, rehabilitation is effective and better than repair.

Various causes are there which need structural rehabilitation such as poor construction practice, unexpected seismic loading condition, design inadequacy, environment degradation, increase in load, lack of maintenance in addition to corrosion induced distress.

Fig. 1.12 Rehabilitation of RCC Beam-Column Joint

Fig. 1.13 Rehabilitation of Structure Components

1.4.2 SEISMIC RETROFITTING

Seismic rehabilitation is the way or operation to carry up the structural system with its components up to specified seismic performance level and seismic repair is nothing but rehabilitation of failed structure to ensure desirable performance under described seismic action.

There are four common types of seismic rehabilitation methods which are as follows:

a) Public Safety Rehabilitation

b) Structure Survivability

c) Primary Structured Undamaged

d) Structure Unaffected

Where, when any structure is reinforced to reduce loss of lives during earthquake activity, although they may be injured, called public safety rehabilitation. The next level of seismic rehabilitation is designed to ensure the building will endure the earthquake, although may be necessity of significant repairs, called structure survivability. Next type of seismic rehabilitation where the majority of structural damage during earthquake activity should be cosmetic, called primary structure undamaged. Last one is the highest level of seismic rehabilitation chosen for any structure of high economic or cultural value and sometimes these terms can mislead, as no building can be made purely or entirely safe.

1.5 FIBRE REINFORCED POLYMER

Fibre Reinforced Polymer (FRP) is a popular material which normally used in retrofitting or strengthening reinforced concrete structural elements in recent years. It is a composite material made of a polymer matrix reinforced with natural or artificial fibres. Some artificial fibres are like carbon, aramid, glass, basalt and many more natural fibres such as paper, wood, asbestos or synthetic fibres have been also used. FRP provides an excellent and outstanding means strengthening existing reinforced and for rehabilitating, and pre-stressed RCC concrete bridges, buildings and many others. FRP provides and cost-effective, efficient and easy to construct any shape of RCC member whether structure requires strengthening to resist against increased future load such as live or dead load, wind or seismic load, or whether structure has been ruptured or damaged due to the reason of overload, heavy seismic action or deterioration of materials. It designed as advance composite material for RCC construction work to act as flexural and shear, and confinement reinforcement.

The chapter of strengthening with fibre reinforced concrete (FRP) was pioneered by U. Meier from Swiss Federal Laboratories for material and research institute in 1980.

In fibre reinforced polymer, fibre is a thing made up of long filament and the main features of fibres are provide stiffness, ductility, strength and rise up capacity of carrying load, and other structural attributes to structures.

In other words fibre reinforced polymer is composites made of long filament fibre in a polymeric resin and cross-section of continuous FRP composites with schematic representation is shown in figure 1.14.

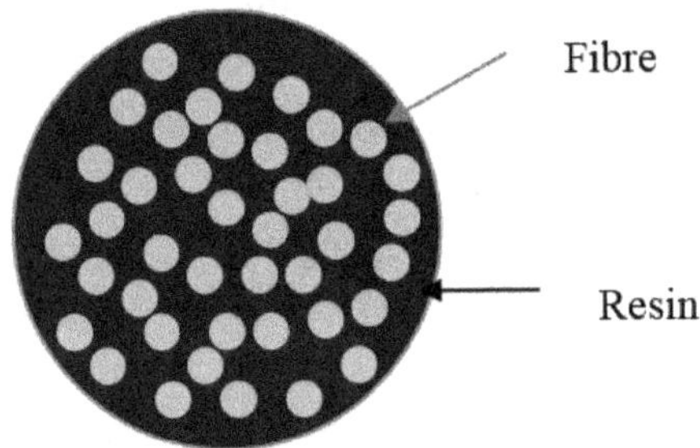

Fig. 1.14 Cross-Section of FRP

Fibres may be of glass, carbon, aramid, polyvinyl alcohol type and many more are used commonly with resin to produce FRP composite. These fibres have great tensile strength as compared steel with short elongation described as below:

a) **Carbon Fibres**: This type of fibre is made up from poly-acrylic nitric and coal pitch or petroleum, and an aggregate of imperfect fine graphite crystals. These fibres are rich in carbon and their attributes depends on the orientation of crystals.

b) **Glass Fibres**: These types of fibres have been used in 1990's which are mainly two types E- glass and alkali-resistant glass fibre.

c) **Polyvinyl Alcohol Fibres**: These type of fibres provide extra elasticity and strength by rolling the fibre during manufacturing process and, are manufactured by polyvinyl-alcohol and higher degree of polymerisation.

d) **Aramid Fibres**: These types of fibres are currently three types which available in market such as Kevlar, Twaron and Technora by name of trade, and these are highly organic type fibres. These are the superstar family in fibre world which are a class of heat-resistant and strong synthetic fibre. The name of fibre comes from a combination of two words, "Aromatic Polyamide". These fibres have excellent attributes such as good resistance to abrasion, no melting point, low flammability, non-conductive, sensitive to ultraviolet radiations as well as acids and salts etc. Due to their superior strength-to-weight ratio and heat-resistant properties, aramid fibres can be used in retrofitting of structural components to improve their strength against seismic activities. Here, these fibres are used in retrofitting or rehabilitation of beam-column joint which is a crucial zone in structure.

1.6 PROPERTIES OF FRP COMPOSITES

1.6.1 MECHANICAL PROPERTIES

Mechanical properties of FRP composites such as compressive strength, flexural strength, tensile strength, modulus of elasticity etc are commonly taken which examine from universal testing machine under monotonic loading. FRP material doesn't exhibit any plastic or yield behaviour before fail when it is loaded under direct tension. Elastic stress-strain relationship as shown in figure 1.15 is used to characterise tensile behaviour of FRP material up to failure point which is sudden or may be catastrophic but strain at rupture stage is much lesser when it compared with that of steel.

Hence, when large ductility or deformation is required in the member as applications, FRP should be used properly with great care. Generally, modulus of elasticity as well as compressive strength of FRP materials is smaller than tension with corresponding values. FRP material can fail easily in fibre micro-buckling, shear failure and tensile failure, under longitudinal compression. However, FRP is not used to rising of compressive stresses or in other word FRP is not recommended to resist compressive stresses as per guidelines of ACI.

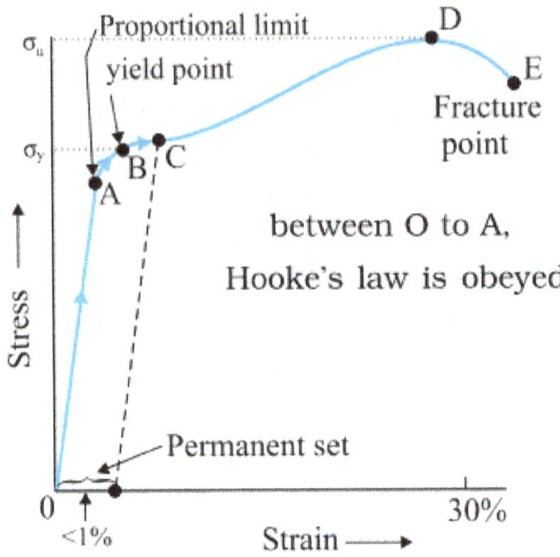

Fig. 1.15 Stress- Strain Relationship

1.6.2 TIME-DEPENDENT BEHAVIOUR

Since three decades, large amount of data on FRP composites or materials regarding fatigue behaviour and creep-rupture, have been generated. Generally, glass fibres and aramid fibres are most susceptible to creep-rupture and fatigue failure as compared to carbon fibres. Due to susceptible of glass fibre on moisture, alkaline and acidic solution, environmental factors play excellent role in fatigue stresses, whereas carbon fibres are unaffected on fatigue strength by the environmental conditions.

1.6.3 DURABILITY

Durability of resin and fibres of various FRP systems is depends on environmental conditions because environmental exposure affects on degrade of mechanical attributes of many FRP's such as acidity, salt water, alkalinity, high temperature, high humidity, thawing and freezing action etc, therefore to study the these adverse environmental conditions on FRP's, many tests are there so that results on resistance of FRP can determine.

2

Categories of Structures

2.1 GENERAL

The term "structure" refers to either the way in which something is ordered or arranged, or the thing itself, that is material in nature. Buildings and machines are examples of man-made material structures, while natural material structures include things like minerals and chemicals as well as living beings. Data structures in computer science and musical form are two examples of abstract structures. A hierarchy (a pyramid of one-to-many interactions), a network (with many-to-many connections), or a lattice (with connections between nearby components) are all examples of possible structures.

The term 'structure' in the context of the construction sector refers to something that is formed or built from multiple interconnected elements with a permanent placement on the ground. It is the responsibility of the structure to preserve the form and design under the effect of external forces. A fundamental principle of structures is that they must be built to resist external loads without shifting and should always be in equilibrium state. Statics is the study of the sources and impacts of static forces acting on stiff objects; and a 'static body' is a construction that is stationary or in equilibrium. The structure must also be able to withstand the most extreme combination of forces that are expected to be applied. This is governed by the structure's location on earth, such as in areas where gusty winds or heavy downpours are typical.

Structural parts, such as beams, columns, slabs, walls, staircases, etc., are the principal load-bearing elements of a structure, and each has its own inherent structural characteristics that must be considered.

Structures are mainly classified in different two categories which include:

- Load Bearing Structure
- Framed Structure

2.2 LOAD BEARING STRUCTURE

A load-bearing structure is one in which walls carry loads to the foundation as shown in figure 2.1. This form of building lacks beams and columns. The load-bearing walls are built on a continuous base known as foundation and are intended to sustain the entire load, including their own weight. Since the ceilings and flooring are supported directly by the walls in a load-bearing structure, the entire weight of the building is transferred to the walls. Walls support roofs, floors, and, of course, one's own weight. Walls distribute weight to the earth through their foundations. Although four stories are possible, this type of structure is practical and cost-effective for up to two stories only. This method of construction is employed where harder strata are available at shallower depths, as the footing of the wall sits directly on them. The walls get notably thicker as the total number of floors increases. This not only reduces the carpet's surface area but also increases the cost.

Instead of load-bearing masonry, the majority of modern buildings are frame structures built of light but highly durable materials that carry floor slabs and have relatively thin and lightweight interior and external walls. The external and internal walls of a load-bearing structure serve as a structural component and a barrier for protection against the elements, including rain, sound, heat, and fire.

Fig. 2.1 A Load Bearing Structure

Historically, this form of structure was favoured for constructing the low-rise structures and modest homes. However, they are hardly utilized today. These structures are appropriate for the construction of only two-story business and residential buildings only. This sort of structure includes structural components that safely transmit and distribute load to the ground, thereby ensuring the building's superior performance and stability.

In modern architecture, there are a variety of load-bearing structures. One should be acquainted with the primary load-bearing structures.

The following is a list of the three main categories of load-bearing structures:

- **Concrete Precast Wall:** As the name suggests, this type of structure is prefabricated, meaning it is manufactured in a controlled environment, let to cure, and then transported to the construction site. This type of wall is simpler to construct, stronger, more significant, and less difficult to maintain.

- **Retaining Wall:** A retaining structure, also known as either a bosom or revetment wall, is a load-bearing structure that helps prevent soil erosion while supporting soil. This wall, unlike most other barriers, is designed to withstand lateral load pressure or retain soil materials.

- **Masonry Fencing:** Among all other load-bearing structures, it provides the most design flexibility. Since it is not prefabricated, any desired height or length can be achieved. It is durable and long-lasting, independent of lateral pressure, resistant to fire, and effective at regulating indoor temperature.

The following analysis procedure determines the load-bearing structures:

- Initially, the entire structure is studied. Thus, each structural element's role is determined.

- The forces exerted by each structural element are determined.

- Both the forces influencing the structural elements and the forces it transmits are determined. These are outside forces.

- Internal forces or static forces are the forces within the structural components.

- The structural element's total structural stability is determined.

- At the end, determine the evidence that the projected building can withstand all the incoming forces.

2.2.1 DETAILS OF LOAD BEARING STRUCTURE

- A load-bearing structure is an element of a building that is designed to safely bear and distribute the load to the subsurface foundation. Walls resist the building's or structure's self-weight, as well as the floor and roof loads.

- The most innovative use of load-bearing is evident in this style of building, and it serves a variety of purposes, such as partitioning the space, sustaining loads, and providing thermal and acoustic protection to the structure, etc.

- This sort of structure prohibits punching holes in walls to link two rooms, as doing so could cause structural damage.

- The massive weight of the walls binds the structure together and stabilises it against external pressures such as wind and earthquake.

Now that you've developed a solid grasp of load-bearing construction, now let us understand the distinction between load-bearing and framed structures. Load-bearing structures are distinguished from framed ones by the presence of components that sustain the weight of the building and transmit it to the ground below. The walls of a load-bearing structure bear the weight of the building, while the columns and beams of a framed building do so.

2.2.2 ADVANTAGES OF LOAD BEARING STRUCTURE

- The load-bearing structure or building is the construction method where loads of buildings, such as the building's weight itself and the living loads, are transmitted to the foundation through walls, ensuring efficiency and the building's stability.

- A load-bearing structure is one that safely transmits the building's weight to the foundation below. The weight of the structure itself, the weight of the ceiling, and the weight of the floor are all supported by the walls.

- This structural structure exemplifies the best use of load-bearing in that it performs many functions, including maintaining loads, isolating the space, shielding the building from sound and heat and so on.

- The destruction of a load-bearing wall to connect two rooms would compromise the structural integrity of the building.

- The massive weight of the walls aids to the structure's stability against external forces such as earthquakes and wind.

2.2.3 DISADVANTAGES OF LOAD BEARING STRUCTURE

Load-bearing buildings have limited use in the building and construction industry due to their disadvantages. Examples include:

- This load-bearing structure is ideal for three-story buildings.

- A load-bearing masonry structure takes more time and labour to build than an equivalent structure built with a different method.

- A lack of adequate thermal protection from the elements is a major drawback of masonry construction.

- After work has begun, the location of the walls cannot be altered.

- The combined weight of the building's brick walls makes the building bulkier overall.

- Compared to frame buildings, unreinforced components are incapable of withstanding strong tensile and shear stresses, resulting in inadequate resilience of brick wall or poor performance against seismic loads.

2.3 FRAMED STRUCTURE

A framed structure as shown in figure 2.2, regardless of its material, is one in which the framework serves as a rigid support system that doesn't need to rely on the floors or walls to prevent it from bending or buckling. Framing members should be made of a material that is robust in both tension and compression, such as wood, steel, or reinforced concrete. Framing does not include masonry skeletons since they cannot be made strong without walls. From prehistoric times until the middle of the nineteenth century, the most popular building style in eastern Asia and northern Europe was the massive wood frame, in which huge posts are set relatively far apart to support thick floor and rooftop beams. The American light wood frame also known as balloon frame, which replaced the framed wood structure, was made up of several closely spaced, small pieces of wood that could be handled with more ease and erected more swiftly using nails than the traditional joinery and dowelling. Since both are founded on the post-and-lintel system, their construction is very similar. The sill (base part) is fastened to the post and the post is set into a flat, watertight foundation made of masonry or concrete. The floors of the top stories are set on crossbeams, which are supported by horizontal elements attached to the building's outside wall. Additionally, the beams are supported by the inside walls.

The heavy-timber system's sturdier beams allow the upper level and roof to extend out of the plane of the foundation posts, providing more headroom and better protection from the elements. Typically, the members are exposed to the outside. In China, Korea, and Japan, the gaps between walls are contained by light screen walls, but in northern Europe, the spaces between walls are partially enclosed by thin bracing members and partially by planks, panels, or (in semi-timbered construction) brickwork or dirt.

For weather protection, the light frame is sheathed with horizontal or vertical boards or shingles that are joined or overlapped. Sheathing aids in bracing and protecting the frame, so this frame is not structurally fully independent as in steel frame structures. Since its introduction, the light-frame technology has not been greatly developed, and it has fallen behind other recent systems. Prefabricated panels intended to lower the rising cost of building have not gained widespread acceptance. Modern laminated-wood and heavy timber processes , however, enable the manufacture of composite members for arches and trusses that can compete with steel construction for certain major projects in wood-rich regions.

Steel framing is founded on the same concepts as wood framing, but the material's significantly superior strength allows for more rigidity with few elements. The load-bearing capability of steel is sufficient for structures that are far higher than those built from other materials, because the beam and column are welded or riveted together, stresses are shared between them, allowing both to be longer and lightweight than in constructions where the beam and column function independently as post and lintel. Thus, vast cubic areas can be covered by four beams and four columns, and buildings of virtually any size can be constructed by connecting cubes along their height and width. Curtain walls, concrete, or even paint are sometimes used to hide the skeleton to prevent corrosion of the structural steel. Large spans in single story buildings are possible with a steel frame, thus it's not just for multi-story structures. Covering systems including trusses, arches, and other elements in an infinite number of forms can be used instead of the standard cube shape to better serve the building's intended purposes.

The section on materials explains how reinforced concrete differs from steel frames. While concrete frames are more adaptable due to their greater rigidity and continuity, steel is favoured for extremely tall constructions due to its lower cost and smaller footprint. This style of construction extends the post-and-lintel principle into three dimensions. One example is box frame construction, in which each unit is made of two walls carrying a slab. Here, again, concrete transcends the barriers that divided ancient ways of construction.

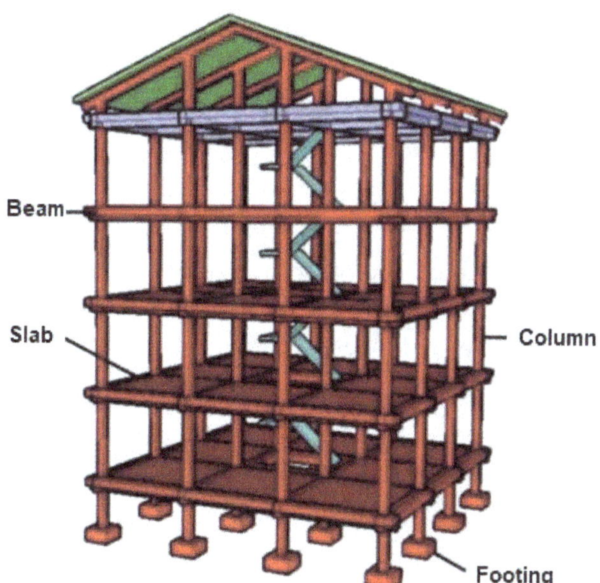

Fig. 2.2 A Frame Structure

There are several points to be noted of framed structures, which are:

a) **Fast Construction:** According to the definition, loads are transferred by structural components such as slabs, columns, beams, and Footings. Consequently, these structural parts can be built up to the upper floors regardless of other processes such as block work, plastering, and finishing works etc. If these activities are well-organized, framed structures can be erected at an astounding rate. In building projects, proper project planning is essential and plays a very important role.

b) **Low Cost of Construction:** The expense of a project is directly proportionate to its duration. Therefore, a considerable reduction in project length might result in a significant decrease in project costs.

c) **Variable Factor of Safety:** Depending on their location, the safety factor of structural elements can vary. The structural members can be constructed for maximum safety based on their placement, so minimizing the needless consumption of materials, which eventually influences the project's cost and length.

d) **Better Utilization of Space:** In framed constructions, the walls do not support any structural loads. Consequently, the width of walls can be changed as desired. In addition, the location of the wall can also be altered at any time during the project's lifetime, allowing the end-user to make adjustments according to their needs.

Framing refers to give support and shape to a building by combining different members in structure. Consequently, a framed structure is a construction composed of beams, columns, and slabs to resist gravitational force and other lateral loads. These structures are typically employed to counteract the enormous forces and moments generated by the imposed loads.

Typical building frames consist of columns and beams that are either fastened or connected, similar to trusses. There are two and three-dimensional frames. The frames can be made of any material, including RCC, steel, and wood. In a framed building, the weight of floors, roofs, and partition walls are carried by beams, which transfer these stresses to the columns. The path of load transfer in a framed structure is from floor to beam, then beam to column, and then further from column to foundation, i.e. the ground.

A wall is a framed construction member whose height and length are greater than its thickness. Walls that withstand vertical loads are known as load-bearing walls. Non-load-bearing walls or partition walls are walls that are subject to no loads except than their own weight, such as enclosure or panel walls. Shear walls are walls whose principal role is to resist horizontal loads. The walls of a framed structure are typically non-load bearing, with the exception of shear walls.

Reinforced concrete, non-load-bearing walls, commonly categorised as partitions, panels, or cross walls, could be prefabricated or cast in place. When prefabricated, panels serve only as exterior cladding are typically linked to the floors or columns of a frame, supported by grade beams, or spanning and supported by between foundations, functioning as both grade beams and walls. As substructures, cast-in-place cross walls are most frequently used.

Panel walls can be replaced by cladding panels. Cladding generally refers to the thin sheets used to encapsulate the framework. The wall cladding may be comprised of corrugated galvanised iron sheets, asbestos cement sheets, thin concrete slabs, copper sheets, glass or wood panels, tiles, etc.

2.3.1 ADVANTAGES OF FRAME STRUCTURE

- Due to its basic design, rapid construction is possible. It can be built more quickly than conventional walled constructions. As primary structural elements, only beams and columns (or a portion of the floor slab) are present in such structures. It is feasible to simultaneously carry out multiple building construction tasks, such as the construction of the higher levels' framework and the completion of the lower floors. Therefore, it is simple to construct a framed structure rapidly

- Greater structural durability and steadiness.

- A building's height is not a limitation, hence multi-story buildings are possible.

- A framed building has more stability and less susceptibility to shaking. Framed buildings are particularly well-suited to seismic regions and industrial settings due to their ability to resist vibrations.

- Framed buildings are extremely sturdy and stable. Framed buildings can withstand large vertical (dead load) and lateral (wind, earthquake) loads without significantly deforming or bending. Dead load is reduced due to absence of thick load bearing walls etc.

- Every completed floor slab acts as a cover to shield the lower floors against rain and sun.

- A framed building offers greater floor space without obstruction between columns. A beam supports a non-load-bearing wall between two columns and a beam above it. This indicates that the maximum height of a wall is equivalent to the height of a story. So, this type of building necessitates thin panels, which enhance the floor area. Nonetheless, the exterior walls should be substantial enough to endure the elements.

- Versatile use of space, no need to build walls above walls, as well as any wall can be moved to any location; consequently, flexibility of usage.

- Adaptable to nearly any form.

- Within the boundaries of the frame, framed buildings can be modified easily. The position of the panel wall can be altered at any time to match the requirements. Hence, increased planning flexibility is readily achievable.

- In framed structures, offsite preparation is possible, particularly for prefabricated construction employing structural steel elements or precast concrete.

- Appropriate distribution of natural light - it is simple to install window openings in walls.

- Due to simple geometry, i.e., simple methods of analysis, it is easy to analyse and design the structures, including computer-aided designs.

- Compared to conventional walled structures, these structures are more suited and cost-effective on filled and soft terrain.

- This type of construction categorises building elements into two distinct groups: load-bearing and non-load-bearing. The construction of non-load-bearing elements is possible with inexpensive materials.

- The strength and stability of the structures have improved.

- The strength and durability of framed structures are exceptionally high. Large dead loads, wind loads, together with earthquakes, do not cause significant deformation or movement in framed structures.

- Framing reduces a structure's tendency to shake. The resistance of framed structures to vibrations makes them suitable for earthquake-prone regions and industrial sites.

A frame structure utilises columns, beams, and slabs to withstand and transfer gravity and other horizontal and transverse stresses safely to the base. The walls fill in the gaps created by the framing structure. The walls are only burdened with their own weight. It is not engaged in the mechanism for load transmission.

2.3.2 FEATURES OF FRAMED STRUCTURES

- Frame structures are a combination of slabs, beams, and columns designed to withstand the massive forces and moments generated by gravity and lateral stresses.

- They comprise a concrete or steel framework that collects the weight and transports it to the foundation in a safe manner.

- The structural elements of the frame are joined using either pinned or fixed connections.

- Wall construction is utilised to fill the space created by the framed structural system. These walls may be load-bearing or nonload-bearing. The majority of the load-bearing walls in the framed construction are shear walls.

- Hence, the primary structural or load-bearing components of a framed structure are columns, shear walls (load bearing ones), beams and slabs.

- A framed construction may be composed of RCC (Reinforced Cement Concrete), wood, or steel, among other materials.

- A frame structure consists of a carefully constructed assemblage of beams, slabs, and columns that can endure the enormous stresses and moments created by intense lateral and gravitational loads.

- They assemble to form a concrete or steel framework that supports the load and delivers it to the foundation without incident.

- The resulting area or cavity is enclosed by walls in a framed structural framework. Here, there are load-bearing and non-load-bearing walls two types of walls. The majority of the loads bearing walls in the framed structure are shear walls.

2.3.3 PRINCIPLES OF FRAMED STRUCTURES

A framed structure is a structure constructed by joining a succession of vertical and horizontal structural parts in the appropriate positions. Columns and beams make up the majority of the framed constructions. At the floor and ceiling levels, beams join columns. Walls split the levels into required-sized rooms and passageways.

The walls may be partition or load-bearing walls. Steel, wood, or reinforced cement concrete (RCC) may be utilized for frame buildings. Lightweight frame structures are made of wood, steel, or reinforced concrete, while multi-story frame structures are made of mild steel. Beams sustain the entire weight of floors, roofs, and dividing walls, transferring these loads to the columns. These columns transmit the entirety of the structure's weight to the foundation.

The steel framework generally sustains all types of loads. All columns, beams, and girders in this type of framed construction are made of steel section. These constructions require adequate bracing to withstand the wind and seismic effects. If the structure is a building, fireproof and other lightweight materials are employed for partitions and external walls. Steel-framed constructions can support more loads inside a given area. In constructions with a steel framework, round or curved work must be avoided.

Reinforced cement concrete also known as RCC is the ideal material for framed constructions if it is designed and constructed appropriately. As was previously said, beams and columns are interconnected to form a grid of girders and beams. To support multiple floor levels, the slabs are constructed monolithically. Based on the type of soil and the foundation's weight, the foundations may consist of isolated or integrated footing, a raft, or a mat.

2.3.4 CONSTRUCTION OF FRAMED BUILDINGS

The following are considerations that must be made during the construction of Reinforced Cement Concrete (RCC) buildings:

- RCC frames are composed of columns, beams, and slabs. Monolithic structure reduces deflection and bending moments, resulting in cost-effective construction. Additional safety precautions are taken.

- A typical RCC frame consists of beams, slabs (as roof or as floor), and columns. In the event of long spans, supplementary beams that span across the main beams might be included to improve load distribution.

- The figure following depicts a typical RCC multi-story building's framework. It demonstrates the monolithic structure of columns, beams, slabs, and girders.

- The concrete process is identical to that of other structures. Yet, a sequential process must be followed. Here, the formwork for the various parts to be cast is initially installed or built. The reinforcement required is then put and concreted. Once the concrete has reached sufficient strength, the formwork is removed.

- The next element to be produced is taken up, and formwork and concrete are applied. Columns are typically constructed first, followed by beams, cross beams, and then slabs.

- As the construction cannot be completed in one continuous stretch, building joints must be given at intervals. In addition, the joints in framed construction should be at the point of least shear.

- The height of the columns is concreted to ensure a correct overlap with the beams and columns on upper stories.

2.4 TYPES OF FRAMES

Depending on the building material, there are fundamentally three types of frames:

- Steel Frame
- Concrete Frame
- Wooden Frame

2.4.1 STEEL FRAME

These structures are composed of a steel framework that carries all loads as shown in figure 2.3. These buildings' columns, beams, and girders are built of steel pieces. These structures must be sufficiently braced to withstand wind and earthquake effects. Generally, fire-resistant and other lightweight materials are chosen for the partitioning and outside walls of these structures. Thus, steel-framed structures are comparable to RCC-framed structures. Steel, being considerably stronger than all types of brickwork, is capable of supporting significantly more weight in a given area. Thus, fewer columns can be correctly placed to give support for beams passing between them, resulting in huge column-free areas.

In mild steel-framed constructions, curving or circular work is avoided as much as possible. Beginning with the basement foundation, supporting columns for upper-floor loads and the roof should be continuous. They should be positioned to directly support the girders holding massive walls. The girders must be directly attached to the columns. It is important to abstain the use of eccentric loading and skew frames. Members that are subjected to bending should be placed as deeply as possible in the direction of the maximum bending moment in order to achieve optimal efficiency. To the greatest extent practicable, the cleats should be set in such a way that the majority of the riveting may be done in the workshop.

Fig. 2.3 A Steel Framed Building

Fig. 2.4 Under-Construction Concrete Framed Building

2.4.2 CONCRETE FRAME

The RCC framed structure as shown in figure 2.4, is made up of a number of frames that are constructed by joining beams and columns at roof and floor levels to create a lattice of the girders and beams. These frames make up the skeleton of the RCC framed structure. Within these frames, the walls are created. At the junction, the slab, girders, and column are built as one solid piece and are rigidly connected to one another. Therefore, in a framed building, the weight of the roofs, floors, and walls are sustained by the girders and beams, which subsequently carry these stresses to the column below and then finally to the foundations.

RCC frames are almost always built using a monolithic construction method, which enables full continuity to be maintained throughout the columns, beams, and slabs of the structure. The primary benefits of continuous construction are decreased bending moment and deflections in the members, which leads to the economical construction of buildings that are suitable in terms of safety.

All throughout the world, framed structures are built due to their multiple advantages. Since 1960, reinforced concrete has become a prevalent material in frame construction. Potentially new building approaches, such as composite construction and space frame technology, are currently being used and will alter the appearance of buildings in the future.

Fig. 2.5 Under-Construction Wooden Framed Building

2.4.3 WOODEN FRAME

Wood provides a number of benefits, including aesthetic appeal, adaptability, longevity, a high strength-to-weight ratio, low thermal inductance, superior electrical insulation, and exceptional strength at relatively low temperatures. It has a huge capacity for shock absorption. It can bear enormous weights for brief periods of time. It may be easily bent into severe curves. It is capable of receiving a variety of ornamental and protective coatings. When frames made of wood are utilised, walls are often constructed with 40cm center-to-center spacing between thin studs as shown in figure 2.5.

Façades, such as wall board and sheathings, floor underlayment and roof sheathing, are typically supplied in the correct widths for attachments to joists, rafters, and studs with the appropriate spacing. Typically, timer studs are installed in partitions and walls with wide faces that are perpendicular to the wall or partition face. The studs are fastened to the sole plate at the bottom and to a combination of horizontal rafters at the top. They may indeed be supported by the top plate or by a rib band header. Typically, wood-bearing wall structures are braced to either a balloon frame or a platform frame.

2.5 COMPARISONS OF STRUCTURES

Structure refers to a collection of interrelated components that are together to serve a particular important purpose. Many structural models exist, including framed, solid, membrane, shell, cables, trusses and arches, surface structure, etc. Due to their geometry, these are primarily classed based on their resistance to different sorts of loads. It is the structure's geometrical configuration that determines its load-bearing capacities. Modern architecture's most common configurations are frames and walls. These walls are commonly referred to as framed and load-bearing walls.

Fig. 2.6 Comparison of Load Bearing and Frame Structure

In a framed construction, a framework or "skeleton" of columns and beams is utilised to transfer various loads to the foundations. In small (often single-story) structures, the framework may be comprised of wood or even aluminium. Typically, the framework is composed of steel or reinforced cement concrete.

In the load-bearing structure, the load-bearing element is the wall itself. These load-bearing walls are often constructed of brick, but reinforced concrete can also be used for the same. Here, the walls are responsible for transferring loads to the base. The primary distinction between a load-bearing structure and a framed building is the responsibility of the members to carry and transfer the load to the foundation as shown in figure 2.6. In a load-bearing structure, the load-bearing members are the walls, but in a framed structure, they are the beams and columns.

The contrasts between load-bearing structures and framed structures are outlined below in table 2.1:

Table 2.1 Comparison Study of Load Bearing Structure and Framed Structure

S. No.	Discussion able Points	Load Bearing Structure	Frame Structure
1	Definition	According to the author of the Building Design and Construction Handbook, Frederick S. Merritt, the load bearing structure is probably the oldest and most common type of structure. This is the type of structure in which the weight of the roofs as well as lateral loads such as earthquakes, winds, etc. are borne by walls, and through walls, and then are transferred to lower floors and eventually to foundations. In some areas, it is also referred to as the wall bearing structure.	A framed structure is one that has a combination of structural components, such as columns, beams, and slabs, all of which are connected to one another in order to withstand gravitational and other lateral loads. In most cases, these structures are employed in an effort to counteract the significant forces and moments that are developed as a result of the imposed loads. In some circles, it is also referred to as a beam column construction.
2	Components	Heavy masonry walls made of brick or stone serve as the load bearing structure of the building. These walls provide support for the entire structure.	Column, beam, and slab make up the components of a framed structure.

3	Load Transfer Path	The vertical load transfer path in load-bearing structures is from slab/floor to walls and from walls to load-bearing footing, i.e. soil.	The vertical weight transfer path in a framed building is from slab/floor to beams, beams to columns, and columns to load-bearing footings and eventually to earth.
4	Height of Structure	Only low-rise structures may be developed. According to "SP 62" (S & T, 1997, Handbook on Building Construction Practices), up to six-story load-bearing structures have been constructed to date. In a few of nations, even 14-story structures have been constructed only of masonry.	Any height of multi-story structures can be developed. According to 'R. Chudley' (Author of Building Construction Handbook), these structures are often constructed for office, hotel, and residential apartment use and include the means of vertical circulation in the form of staircases and lifts comprising up to 20% of the floor space.
5	Resistant to Earthquake	As a result of their construction with masonry units, such as stone and brick, load-bearing structures have low earthquake resistance. (If not	As the frame's columns, beams, and slabs function as a single unit, framed structures are more stiff and earthquake-resistant. Yet, the horizontal load route

		performed properly.) Nonetheless, its performance for low-rise buildings is similar. It requires precise designs and details.	must be precisely defined, developed, and documented.
6	Thickness of Wall	Thicker walls	Thinner walls.
7	Walls Construction	There are no beams or columns in a load-bearing system. Walls must therefore be constructed initially.	Walls are built in framed structures after the frame is complete.
8	Carpet Area	Because the walls in these sorts of structures are thicker, there is less usable carpet surface, which reduces the planning efficiency of carpet area.	When the walls are thinner, there is more carpet space accessible in these buildings.
9	Popularity	Currently uncommon form of construction. The first kind of structure known to civilization is load-bearing walls.	The most common type of building now-a-days.
10	Excavation Required	More excavation is required in these types of structures.	Less excavation is required in framed structures.

11	Labour Required	It is more labor intensive.	It is less labor intensive, but it needs skilled labour.
12	Speed of Construction	Slow speed of construction.	Fast speed of construction.
13	Material Required	It needs more material. Hence, dead load is greater. Less steel and cement are used.	It requires less material. More steel and cement are used.
14	Repair Cost	The repair and maintenance cost of load-bearing structures is lower.	The repair and maintenance cost of load-bearing structures is more.
15	Life of Structure	Although some rules are not fully adhered to, there is little impact on structure's lifespan.	Life expectancy is decreased if proper procedures are not followed and codes are not rigorously adhered to.
16	Worker Required for Construction	Construction can be done by workers with or without specialized training.	For its construction, only personnel with specialized skills are required.
17	Uniformity of Wall	It is impossible to keep the wall's thickness uniform across its entirety. The wall's thickness becomes more as the height of the structure grows. As a result, the plan	The wall's thickness can be kept consistent throughout the structure. There is no change to the thickness of the wall as the height increases. Therefore plan dimensions do

		dimensions vary throughout all floors.	not change on higher floor.
18	Purpose/Function of Wall	The purpose of a wall in a load-bearing building is to bear load; as a result, practically all of the walls in the structure are load bearing, with the exception of those that provide privacy and security. A disadvantage is presented by the constraint of wall over wall or room over room. External and interior walls in a load-bearing structural system serve not only as a structural element but also as an enclosure for the purpose of providing protection from the elements, including rain, sound, heat, and fire, among other things.	The walls serve both as privacy and a security measure here. There is no limit of constructing building walls on top of walls and rooms on top of rooms. Both the exterior and the interior walls of a framed structural system serve only the function of creating enclosures, which allows for the formation of rooms and provides protection from the elements.
19	Flexibility in Design	It is inflexible in design, as barriers cannot be removed or relocated, resulting in reduced effectiveness. As	It has a flexible design since wall placement can be altered. It is possible to create more useful architectural design.

		walls are load-bearing components, it is required to build wall upon wall in load-bearing structures. Hence, you cannot alter the location of the wall, which reduces the flexibility of its use.	Flexible space utilization is there. There is no need to build walls on walls. Any wall can be moved to any location. Therefore, flexibility in application.
20	Room Dimension	The dimensions of a room cannot be altered because walls can only be placed over other walls.	The room dimensions are modifiable.
21	Feasibility of Cantilever Elements	Including a Cantilever element into this system is a challenging task. Moreover, it is only permitted for brief spans.	This system makes it simple to implement cantilever elements.
22	Span in Structure	Long spans areas are not conceivable in the case of load-bearing structures. Span limitations, like room sizes are there in these structures.	Long spans areas are feasible for framed structures. There is no restriction on room dimensions.
23	Cost Variation According to Foundation Depth	If the depth of the foundation exceeds 1.5 metres, the foundation cost of a load-bearing building is greater than that of	There is no significant cost rise with increasing foundation depth.

		a framed structure, and can occasionally be more expensive than an RCC-framed structure.	
24	Flexibility in Construction	The construction of a load-bearing structure is a time-consuming and difficult process, especially for buildings designed to withstand earthquakes.	Building of a framed building is straightforward, on the other hand.
25	Materials for Construction	Stone, brick, concrete block, and other similar materials can all be used to construct load-bearing walls.	The frame may be made of RCC, steel, wooden, or any number of other materials.
26	Opening in Wall	In this type of construction, there are constraint on the ability to provide openings in walls that will have a significant impact on the amount of ventilation and light in the room.	It is feasible to create large openings in walls in this type of construction.
27	Design Complexity	The load-bearing structure design is basic and simple.	The design of framed structures is not as straightforward as that of load-bearing structures. One

			requires design expertise and software tools.
28	Plant & Machines for Construction	Unlike framed structures, load-bearing structures can be created without expensive equipment and machinery. The framework is an active structural component, and as all components are essential, any modification to the frame could compromise the safety of the entire structure. But, walls are modifiable.	The construction of framed structures requires expensive machinery and equipment.
29	Carpet Area Efficiency	If the price of the land is particularly high, the savings coming from a lower building cost will be nullified because the useable carpet area will be smaller. Therefore increased construction rate and expense per square foot of carpeted area.	As the carpet area efficiency is greater, framed structure is not only efficient but also cost effective, especially when the land prices in urban areas are high.
30	Use of Construction	When appropriate foundation soil is	It is mostly utilized for high-rise and low-

	Based on Load Bearing Capacity of Soil	available between 1.2 and 1.5m, this type of construction is employed for low-rise constructions. Frederick S. Merritt, author of the Building Design and Construction Handbook, argues that the weight of the load-bearing walls makes such design impractical for very high buildings. Yet, tall buildings could benefit from a wall bearing system if it is constructed with reinforcing steel. Only on hard strata can it be built.	rise structures where good soil quality for load-bearing foundations is unavailable, often up to 1.5 to 2.0m, and where bricks are also more expensive. It can be built on any soil type, including black cotton soil, reclaimed dirt, and soft soil.
31	Time for Completion	Walls must be constructed first since they support the slab or roof; hence, all walls must be constructed simultaneously, which is time-consuming.	Typically, the RCC-framed structure is created first, followed by the external and interior walls, resulting in greater speed.
32	Strength of Masonry Unit Required	As the ultimate load-bearing materials, bricks with a compressive strength of at least 75 kg/cm^2,	Bricks with the lowest allowable compressive strength may be used for infill walls because their

		as determined by local building requirements, are necessary.	structural significance is negligible.
33	Alteration of Structural Element	While walls are the active structural elements, they cannot be altered at any time. One cannot alter walls.	Because the frame is a active structural element and because every component is crucial, modifying the frame could compromise the integrity of the entire structure. But you can change the walls if you want to.

In conclusion, load-bearing structures are much more cost-effective than framed ones. This is true, however, only if the cost of bricks for load-bearing walls is low in comparison to the cost of concrete for beams and columns in framed buildings, and if the foundation is no more than 1.00m to 1.2m deep. R.C.C. framed structure is always preferred when the structures are vast, where you require flexibility in design (i.e., you don't want a wall over wall), and when there are large span structures, because load bearing structures have many restrictions. It is only cost-effective to build a load-bearing structure if the necessary bricks and stones can be acquired quickly and at a low cost. The cost of a load-bearing structure may skyrocket or be less competitive with a framed construction in a location where clay for bricks is difficult to come by. The cost of a load-bearing structure goes up proportionally to its height since the thickness of its walls must grow as the building gets taller.

3

Construction Materials

3.1 GENERAL

The term "construction materials" refers to any substance or item used in the construction or renovation of buildings, infrastructure, or other structures. These substances may be natural, synthetic, or a combination of the two. They are chosen according to their physical and chemical qualities, durability, cost-effectiveness, and aesthetic appeal.

Here are some of the most common construction materials:

- **Concrete:** This material is composed of cement, water, and aggregates (sand, gravel, or crushed stone). Due to its strength, durability, and adaptability, it is one of the most commonly used construction materials. Concrete is utilised for the construction of foundations, walls, floors, and bridges.

- **Steel:** Steel is an iron-carbon alloy famous for its strength, durability, and corrosion resistance. It is typically employed in the construction of high-rise buildings, bridges, and other structures requiring a high load-bearing capacity.

- **Wood:** Wood is a natural building material that is frequently utilised for structural and ornamental purposes. It is adaptable, renewable, and can be sourced responsibly. Typically, wood is utilised for building structures, flooring, and decorative finishes.

- **Brick:** Bricks are a common building material for walls, pavements, and aesthetic purposes, produced from clay or concrete. They are recognised for their resilience, fire resistance, and aesthetic appeal.

- **Glass:** Glass is a material that can be seen through completely or partially, and it is frequently utilised in the construction of windows, doors, and skylights. In the form of glass walls and facades, it is also employed for decorative purposes in some contexts. Glass is well-known for its attractive appearance, transparency, and ability to efficiently store and transmit light.

- **Asphalt:** Asphalt is a mixture of aggregates and bitumen that is typically utilised for road construction, roofing, and waterproofing. It is renowned for its toughness, flexibility, and weather resistance.

- **Gypsum:** Gypsum is a regularly used mineral for drywall and plaster. It is renowned for its fire resistance, soundproofing, and usability.

Other common building materials are cement, paints, glues, sealants, and insulation materials. Materials are chosen based on the needs of the project, such as cost, durability, and impact on the environment. It's important to choose the right materials for a building project to make sure it's safe, lasts a long time, and meets the requirements.

3.2 BINDING MATERIALS

Binding material is any substance that is used to hold together other materials or parts. Binding materials are used in many different ways, from building and manufacturing to arts and crafts. Binders hold together pigments and sometimes filling material to form paints, pastels, and other materials used for artistic and utilitarian painting. Materials include wax, linseed oil, natural gums such as gum arabic or gum tragacanth, methyl cellulose, or proteins such as egg white or casein.

Some common examples of binding materials and their properties are as follows:

i. **Cement:** Cement is a binding material that is used in construction to hold things together, like bricks, stones, and concrete blocks. It is made by heating limestone, clay, and other minerals to high temperatures, which turns them into a hard, strong substance. When you mix cement with water, a chemical reaction called "hydration" takes place. This makes the cement harden and form a strong bond.

ii. **Adhesives:** Adhesives are materials that are used to stick two or more surfaces together. They can be made from natural or man-made materials and come in different forms like liquid, paste, and tape. Epoxy, cyanoacrylate, and polyurethane are all common types of glue.

iii. **Resins:** Resins are synthetic materials used as binders in numerous applications, such as coatings, adhesives, and composites. They are produced by combining at least two compounds that react to form a hard, durable substance. Polyester, epoxy, and acrylic are three typical forms of resins.

iv. **Clay:** Clay is a popular binding material used in ceramics and pottery. It is created by combining silica, feldspar, and kaolin with high temperatures to form a hard, resilient substance. Clay is frequently used as a binding material because it can be sculpted and moulded into a variety of forms.

v. **Bitumen:** Bitumen is a petroleum-based substance used for binding. It is frequently used in the construction of roads to create a robust, waterproof surface. Mixing bitumen with aggregates such as sand and gravel produces asphalt, which is then applied to the road surface.

vi. **Wire and Twine:** This material can be used to bind things, such as when wrapping goods or tying up various building elements.

Overall, binding materials play a significant role in a variety of industries and are necessary for the production of durable, stable goods. The choice of binding material is dependent on the application, as many materials have distinct qualities that make them suited for particular tasks.

3.2.1 CEMENT- AN IMPORTANT BINDER

Cement is a building substance used for binding different elements together by hardening, setting, and adhering to them, as shown in figure 3.1. It is produced by grinding clinker, which is formed when limestone, clay, and other materials are heated in a kiln.

Named after the English island of Portland, where it was initially manufactured in the 19th century, Portland cement is by far the most used variety. In order to modify the cement's strength and setting time, gypsum and other ingredients are added to the clinker during the manufacturing process.

Fig. 3.1 a) Cement in Powder Form, b) Cement Available in Bags

Cement is utilised in a variety of construction applications, such as the creation of concrete, mortar, and grout. Mixing cement, water, and aggregate (such as sand or gravel) results in a solid mass that can be poured into moulds or used as a building material. Mortar is a mixture of cement, sand, and water used to adhere bricks, stones, or other materials, whereas grout is a mixture of cement, water, and fine sand used to fill the spaces between tiles or masonry units.

Grout is cement, water, and fine sand mixture used to fill the spaces between tiles or masonry components. The grout offers a consistent and sturdy surface, strengthens the building's structural integrity, and improves its overall aesthetic. There are several types of cement used for construction and each type has its own unique properties and uses. Here are some of the most commonly used types of cement:

i. **Ordinary Portland Cement (OPC):** This is the most popular form of cement, used for general construction projects. Clinker and gypsum are ground together to produce OPC.

ii. **Portland Pozzolana Cement (PPC):** This form of cement is produced through the grinding of clinker and pozzolanic elements such as fly ash, volcanic ash, etc. PPC is utilised in the construction of dams, bridges, and other durable constructions.

iii. **Rapid Hardening Cement:** This kind of cement is utilised when a rapid increase in strength is necessary. It is produced by increasing the amount of C_3S in the cement, which provides it with a high initial strength.

iv. **Sulphate Resistant Cement:** This type of cement is employed in construction projects with high sulphate-containing soil or water. It is produced by decreasing the C_3A component of the cement, which confers sulphate resistance.

v. **White Cement:** This form of cement is employed for decorative applications, such as floors and sculptures. During the production process, iron oxide-free limestone is combined with clinker.

vi. **Coloured Cement:** This cement is utilised to impart colour to concrete buildings. It is produced by adding colours to white cement during production.

vii. **Low Heat Cement:** This form of cement is employed in large concrete constructions, such as dams, where the heat created during hydration might lead to thermal cracking. It is produced by decreasing the cement's C_3S and C_3A concentration.

Cement is a vital and flexible building material as shown in figure 3.1, yet it has certain negative environmental effects. Cement manufacture consumes a substantial quantity of energy and generates a substantial amount of greenhouse gas emissions. Efforts have been undertaken in recent years to develop more sustainable varieties of cement and lessen the environmental impact of cement manufacture.

3.3 AGGREGATES

Aggregates are a crucial building element that are utilised extensively in construction. Sand, gravel, crushed stone, and recycled concrete are examples of aggregates that are used with a cementing agent to form concrete or mortar.

Following are some advantages of using aggregates as a construction material:

i. **Strength and durability:** Aggregates give concrete and mortar the strength and durability to endure the strains of heavy loads and weathering.

ii. **Cost-effective:** Aggregates are easily available, which makes them a more economical building material than steel or wood.

iii. **Versatility:** Aggregates are available in various sizes, forms, and hues, making them adaptable for usage in a variety of building applications.

iv. **Fire resistance:** Aggregate-based concrete possesses exceptional fire resistance, making it an appropriate building material for fire-resistant structures, such as bridges and tunnels.

v. **Sustainable:** Aggregates can be made from recycled materials, such as crushed concrete, reducing waste and conserving natural resources.

vi. **Insulation:** With its superior insulating characteristics, lightweight aggregate concrete is suited for construction in colder areas.

In summary, aggregates are a versatile, cost-effective, and durable building material that is widely used in construction.

Fig. 3.2 Course Aggregates Retained on 4.75mm Sieve

Fig. 3.3 Fine Aggregates Passing through 4.75mm Sieve

3.3.1 TYPES OF AGGREGATES

Coarse and fine aggregates are two categories of construction-related aggregates. They are often combined in concrete mixtures to give bulk, stability, and strength and are categorised according to their particle size. The following is a brief summary of each form of aggregate:

i. **Coarse aggregates:** Coarse aggregates are bigger particles with diameters ranging from 3/8 to several inches as shown in figure 3.2. They are typically composed of crushed rocks or gravel and are used to provide concrete mixtures volume and strength. Construction projects such as roads, bridges, and building foundations frequently employ coarse aggregates.

ii. **Fine aggregates:** Fine aggregates are tiny particles ranging in size from one-fourth of an inch to dust as shown in figure 3.3. Often composed of sand, crushed stone, or gravel screens, they are used to fill the spaces between bigger aggregates in concrete mixtures. Fine aggregates are frequently employed in construction projects like sidewalks, driveways, and building floors.

In concrete mixtures, the blend of coarse and fine particles strikes a balance between workability and durability. The coarse aggregates contribute bulk and strength to the mixture, while the fine aggregates aid to create a more homogeneous mixture by filling the spaces between the bigger particles. The aggregates used in a project are determined by a number of parameters, including the intended strength, durability, and aesthetics of the finished result.

3.4 FLY ASH

Fly ash is produced when coal is burned in power plants. Fly ash is comprised of microscopic, light particles that are transported up the chimney by the exhaust gases produced when coal is burned. Electrostatic precipitators or baghouses are used to collect fly ash from the power plant's exhaust gases before the tiny particles are released into the sky. Once collected, fly ash can be utilized in numerous ways, including as a partial replacement for cement in the manufacturing of concrete, as a soil supplement, and as a component in the creation of bricks and other building materials.

Fly ash is called "green" since it is a recycled waste product that would otherwise be dumped in landfills. Yet, it may include trace levels of heavy metals, necessitating cautious handling and disposal to avoid potential environmental repercussions.

3.5 BRICKS

Bricks have been a common building material for many years and are still used often in new construction as shown in figure 3.4. Here are a few explanations:

i. **Durability:** Bricks are recognised for their durability and can be manufactured of clay or concrete. They are resistant to fire, water, and pests and can tolerate harsh weather conditions.

ii. **Low maintenance:** Bricks are a cost-effective solution because they require very little maintenance. They do not need to be polished, sealed, or treated, so they can last for decades without revealing wear and tear.

iii. **Energy efficiency:** Due to their high thermal mass, bricks can retain and absorb heat. This makes them energy-efficient solutions as they can assist manage a building's temperature, thereby decreasing the demand for heating and cooling systems.

iv. **Aesthetics:** Bricks are available in numerous colours, sizes, and textures, making them an adaptable building material. They can be utilised to produce a variety of architectural styles, ranging from traditional to contemporary.

v.   **Sustainability:** Bricks are created from natural substances and are recyclable till the end of their lifespan. In addition, they have a long lifespan, which decreases the need for replacement and the environmental effect connected with it.

Fig. 3.4 Burnt Clayey Bricks

Bricks are a sustainable, long-lasting, low-maintenance, energy-efficient, aesthetically attractive, and energy-efficient building material. There are numerous varieties of bricks utilised in construction.

Here are some common varieties of bricks:

i. **Burnt Clay Bricks:** They are the most popular sort of kiln-fired bricks created from clay. They have excellent durability and compressive strength.

ii. **Fly Ash Bricks:** These bricks are created by combining fly ash, cement, and water. They are lightweight and provide excellent thermal insulation.

iii. **Concrete Bricks:** This brick is composed of cement, sand, and water. They are useful for load-bearing structures due of their high compressive strength.

iv. **Engineering Bricks:** These bricks are manufactured specifically for use in civil engineering projects like bridges and tunnels. They are extremely durable and water-repellent.

v. **Sand Lime Bricks:** These bricks are created by combining sand, lime, and water. They are useful for load-bearing walls due of their high compressive strength.

vi. **Fire Bricks:** These fire clay-made bricks are utilised to line fireplaces, ovens, and furnaces. They are extremely resistant to heat and can sustain high temperatures.

vii. **Hollow Bricks:** The hollow core of these bricks makes them lightweight and manageable. They are employed for non-load-bearing walls and as filler for reinforced concrete constructions.

viii. **CSEB Bricks:** Compressed Stabilized Earth Bricks are created by compressing a mixture of soil, sand, and cement. They are environmentally friendly and have excellent insulating characteristics.

3.6 CONCRETE

Concrete is a mixture of cement, water, fine and coarse aggregates, and often other materials such as fly ash, slag, and admixtures, as shown in figure 3.5. It is a versatile building material that is used for a wide range of construction applications, including building foundations, walls, floors, bridges, roads, and dams. The cement in concrete is typically Portland cement, which is made by grinding clinker, a mixture of limestone, clay, and other materials, and adding gypsum to regulate the setting time. The fine and coarse aggregates are typically sand and gravel or crushed stone, respectively.

Fig. 3.5 Green Concrete

Concrete is an extremely important construction material that is used in a wide variety of applications due to its strength, durability, and versatility. Here are some of the reasons why concrete is so commonly used in construction:

i. **Strength and Durability:** Concrete is known for its strength and durability, which makes it a popular choice for buildings, bridges, roads, and other structures. It can withstand heavy loads, extreme weather conditions, and even fire.

ii. **Versatility:** Concrete can be molded into almost any shape, making it a versatile material that can be used for a wide range of construction projects. It can be cast in place, precast off-site, or even sprayed into place as a liquid.

iii. **Cost-Effective:** Concrete is a relatively low-cost material compared to other building materials like steel or wood. It also requires minimal maintenance over its lifetime, which makes it a cost-effective choice for many construction projects.

iv. **Sustainability:** Concrete is made from natural materials like water, aggregates, and cement, which makes it a sustainable choice for construction. Additionally, concrete can be recycled and reused, reducing waste and conserving resources.

v. **Aesthetics:** Concrete can be finished in a variety of ways, including staining, stamping, and polishing, which allows for a wide range of aesthetic options. This makes it a popular choice for architects and designers who want to create unique and visually appealing structures.

3.7 STEEL

Steel is a popular building material because of its strength, durability, and adaptability. It is utilised in a variety of forms, including steel beams, steel columns, and steel plates, to construct buildings, bridges, tunnels, and other infrastructure. Steel's strength is one of its key advantages as a construction material. Steel is renowned for its high tensile strength, which indicates that it can endure a great deal of stress and strain without breaking or bending. Its durability enables steel constructions to support enormous weights and endure adverse weather conditions.

Steel is also good because it lasts a long time. Steel doesn't rot, warp, or shrink like some other building materials, like wood. This makes it great for long-term use. Steel is also immune to fire, pests, and other types of damage, so it can last for a long time without needing to be fixed or replaced often.

Steel is also very flexible and can be used for many different things. It can be bent and cut to fit different needs, and it can be bolted or welded together to make structures that are very complicated. Because it can be used in so many ways, steel is a great material for architects and engineers who want to make buildings that are both useful and nice to look at.

Steel has many benefits, but there are also some problems with using it as a building material. Steel, for example, is a fairly expensive material that needs specialised tools and skills to work with. Steel structures can also be susceptible to corrosion if they aren't taken care of properly. This can weaken the structure and make it less safe.

Overall, steel is a popular and useful building material that offers builders, architects, and engineers a wide range of benefits. Its strength, durability, and adaptability make it a great choice for a wide range of building projects, from small homes to large infrastructure.

Fig. 3.6 Steel Reinforcement

3.7.1 STEEL REINFORCEMENT

Rebar, which is another name for steel reinforcement, is a common material used to strengthen concrete structures as shown in figure 3.6. Carbon steel is used to make reinforcing steel, which is usually shaped into bars with ridges, bumps, or other changes on the surface to help the steel stick better to the concrete. When steel reinforcement is added to a concrete structure, it makes the structure stronger and lasts longer. Without reinforcement, concrete is strong in compression but weak in tension. Steel reinforcement helps fix this problem by taking on tensile stresses and passing them on to the concrete around it.

Reinforcing steel is extensively utilised in a wide range of concrete constructions, such as bridges, buildings, and parking garages. The size and spacing of the reinforcement bar employed are determined by the design specifications and intended function of the structure. Reinforcement installation is also essential for assuring the strength and integrity of the final concrete construction. Commonly, concrete structures are reinforced with steel to increase their strength and durability. Below are the principal steel reinforcing types:

i. **Mild Steel Reinforcement:** In concrete structures, mild steel reinforcement is a typical type of reinforcement as shown in figure 3.7(a). It is also known as black steel reinforcement and contains between 0.15 and 0.25 percent carbon. This form of reinforcement is commonly utilised in construction because it is readily available, inexpensive, and possesses a high tensile strength. MS bars, also known as mild steel reinforcement bars, are commonly employed to impart tensile strength to concrete buildings. As concrete is poured, it is strong in compression but weak in tension. The addition of MS bars makes the construction stronger and more durable by distributing the tensile stress. MS bars are available in a range of widths and lengths, and they are commonly employed in reinforced concrete constructions such as buildings, bridges, and roads. In addition, they are frequently utilised in precast concrete products like pipes, poles, and heaps.

   Importantly, mild steel reinforcement can corrode over time when exposed to air and moisture. This can lead to structural deterioration if not handled; therefore, concrete structures reinforced with mild steel require correct design, construction, and maintenance to assure their long-term durability.

ii. **High Yield Strength Deformed (HYSD) Bars**: High Yield Strength Deformed (HYSD) bars are a type of building reinforcement bar as shown in figure 3.7(b). They are also known as Tor steel, Thermal Mechanically Treated bars, or TMT bars. The yield strength of these bars is greater than that of mild steel reinforcement bars.

   In order to produce HYSD bars, mild steel bars are subjected to a variety of operations, including quenching and tempering, which increase their strength and ductility. The bars are first hot-rolled into the correct shape, followed by a chilling procedure that modifies the microstructure of the steel. The bars are then treated to additional heat treatment to increase their tensile strength and abrasion resistance. Using HYSD bars in construction gives numerous benefits. They have greater yield strength, meaning they can withstand greater forces before breaking or yielding. This makes them appropriate for use in structures vulnerable to strong loads or seismic activity. In addition, they have superior adhesion to concrete, which increases the overall strength of the building.

iii. **TMT (Thermo Mechanically Treated) Bars**: TMT (Thermo Mechanically Treated) steel reinforcement bars are a form of building reinforcement bar as shown in figure 3.7(c). They are an improvement above conventional HYSD (High Yield Strength Deformed) bars. They are also known as TEMPCORE bars. TMT bars are produced by exposing mild steel bars to a series of operations, such as quenching and tempering, which enhances their strength and ductility. The bars are first hot-rolled into the correct shape, followed by a chilling procedure that modifies the microstructure of the steel. The bars are then treated to additional heat treatment to increase their tensile strength and abrasion resistance. The primary advantage of TMT bars over conventional HYSD bars is their superior tensile strength and ductility. This indicates that they can withstand bigger loads before yielding or breaking, as well as greater deformation prior to breaking. TMT bars are also more resistant to corrosion and have a stronger bond with concrete, which increases the structure's overall strength.

a)

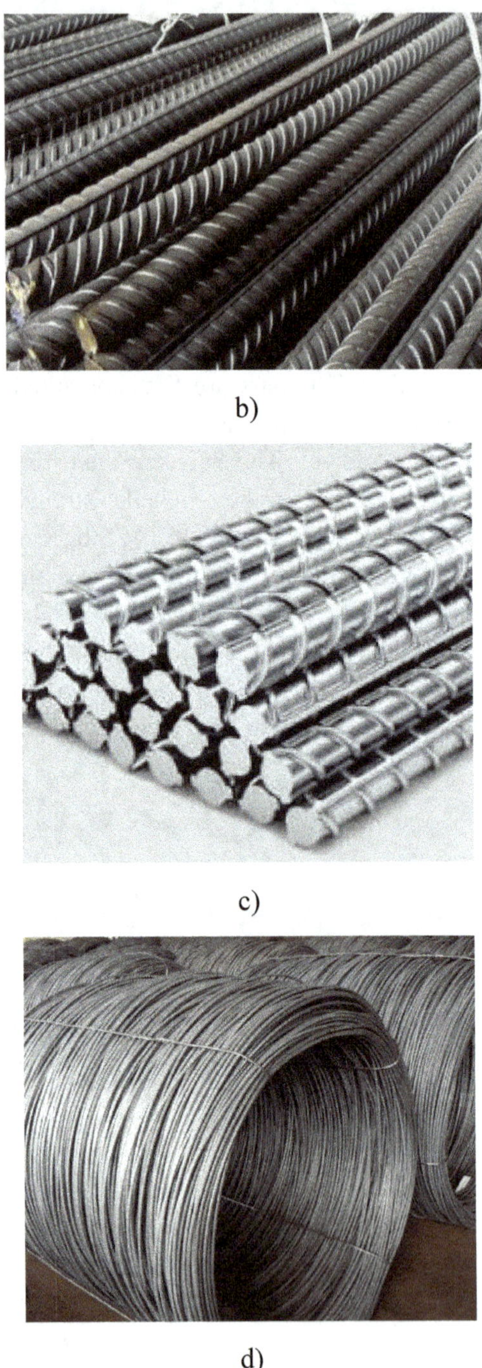

b)

c)

d)

Fig. 3.7 a) Mild Steel, b) HYSD Bars, c) TMT Bars, and d) CRB Steel

iv. **CRB Steel Bars**: Cold Rolled Ribbed (CRB) steel reinforcement bars are a form of building reinforcement bar as shown in figure 3.7(d). They are an enhancement above conventional mild steel reinforcement bars and are also known as Ribbed Bars. The production of CRB bars involves cold rolling a hot-rolled mild steel bar. The method of cold rolling produces a ribbed surface on the bar, which strengthens the bond between the bar and the concrete. The ribs also enhance the bar's surface area, which improves grip and strengthens the bar's bond with the concrete.

3.8 MORTAR

Mortar is a mixture of cement, sand, and water that is used to bind together bricks, stones, and concrete blocks during construction, as shown in figure 3.8. It is often applied between these materials' joints, where it hardens and forms a strong, long-lasting connection. Mortar has been utilised for millennia and is an essential element in the construction of buildings and infrastructures. The composition of mortar might vary depending on its intended purpose and the constituent components. Several varieties of cement, for instance, can be used to produce mortar with differing levels of strength and longevity. Mortar can serve as an aesthetic feature in addition to holding building materials together. By adding pigments or other ingredients to the slurry, various colours and textures can be generated. Overall, mortar plays an important function in the construction industry and is an integral part of many building projects.

Fig. 3.8 Cement Mortar

There are various varieties of mortar depending on the cement, additives, and sand used to create the combination. The following are common types of mortar:

- **Portland cement mortar:** It consists of portland cement, sand, and water, and is the most popular type of mortar. It can be used for the majority of types of masonry building.

- **Lime mortar:** It is composed of lime, sand, and water. Lime mortar is adaptable and can handle the natural movement of building components. It is frequently employed in preservation and restoration operations.

- **Bitumen Mortar:** It is a form of mortar comprised of bitumen and sand. Bitumen, often known as asphalt or tar, is an extremely viscous, sticky, black liquid or semi-solid petroleum compound. Bitumen mortar is frequently employed in waterproofing and paving applications, such as the sealing of roofs, bridges, and roadways. In order to create bitumen mortar, bitumen must first be heated until it becomes liquid. The bitumen is then combined with sand to form uniform slurry. The mixture is placed to the to-be-sealed or paved surface while it is still hot and liquid; as it cools and hardens, it solidifies.

It is very resistant to weathering, chemical assaults, and abrasion. Bitumen mortar has good waterproofing capabilities. Moreover, it is sturdy and has a long life span. However, it may grow fragile with time and should not be used in regions exposed to high temperatures or strong sunlight.

4

COMPONENTS AND JOINTS

4.1 GENERAL

Buildings are complicated constructions that perform multiple functions, including providing shelter and housing and supporting trade and industry. They consist of a variety of components, each of which has a distinct purpose and works together to form a cohesive and functional whole. Fully understanding the various building components is vital for architects, engineers, construction professionals, and anyone engaged in the design, construction, or maintenance of structures.

The components of a building can be broadly divided into structural and non-structural categories. The foundation, framing, walls, floors, and roof are structural components that support and stabilise the building. Non-structural components include plumbing, electricity, HVAC, and other mechanical systems, as well as flooring, paint, and trim.

Each component of a building plays a vital part in guaranteeing the structure's safety, functionality, and aesthetic appeal. Every component, from the foundation that holds the building to the roof that protects it from the weather, must be carefully designed, erected, and maintained to ensure the durability and safety of the structure. Moreover, since building regulations and construction standards continue to advance, it becomes increasingly necessary for building industry professionals to be current on the most recent trends, technologies, and best practises in building design and construction.

4.2 FOUNDATION

A structure's foundation is a key component, whether it is a building, a bridge, or a tower. The foundation provides the required support for the structure to stand solidly and resist loads. This chapter will examine the significance of foundation as a structural component.

The foundation is the lowest portion of a structure that contacts the ground and transfers loads to the earth. It is typically composed of concrete, masonry, or other materials that can withstand the compressive and shear pressures exerted by the structure's weight and the loads it bears.

4.2.1 PURPOSE OF FOUNDATION

The foundation serves various essential roles, including:

i. Supporting the weight of the structure and any loads it carries: The foundation must be capable of supporting and transferring the structure's weight to the earth without settling or shifting.

ii. Evenly distributing the loads: The foundation must evenly distribute the loads throughout the earth to prevent isolated settlements that could cause the structure to tilt or collapse.

iii. Stabilizing the structure: To prevent the structure from collapsing over, the foundation must provide stability against lateral pressures such as wind and seismic activity.

iv. Protecting against soil movement: The foundation must guard against soil movement induced by moisture fluctuations or frost heave that could damage the structure.

4.2.2 TYPES OF FOUNDATION

There are numerous types of foundations used in construction of buildings. The choice of foundation type is determined by factors including soil type, building load, and local building codes. The two primary types of foundations are shallow and deep foundations as shown in figure 4.1.

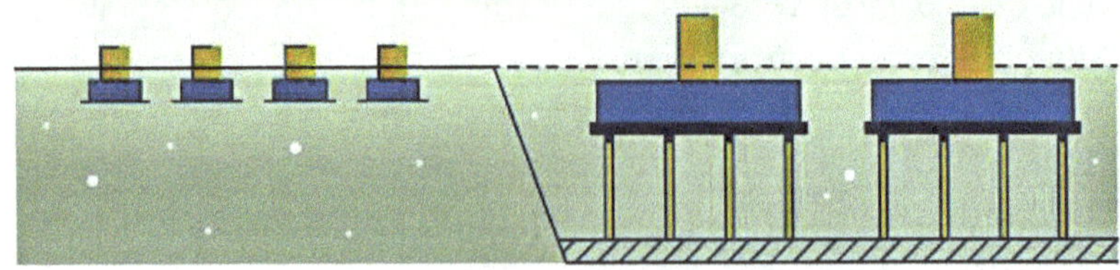

Fig. 4.1 Shallow and Deep Foundation

Shallow foundation: A shallow foundation is a type of foundation used to transfer the loads of a building or other structure to the surface earth. When the soil near the surface is sufficiently robust to support the structure's weight, shallow foundations are often employed.

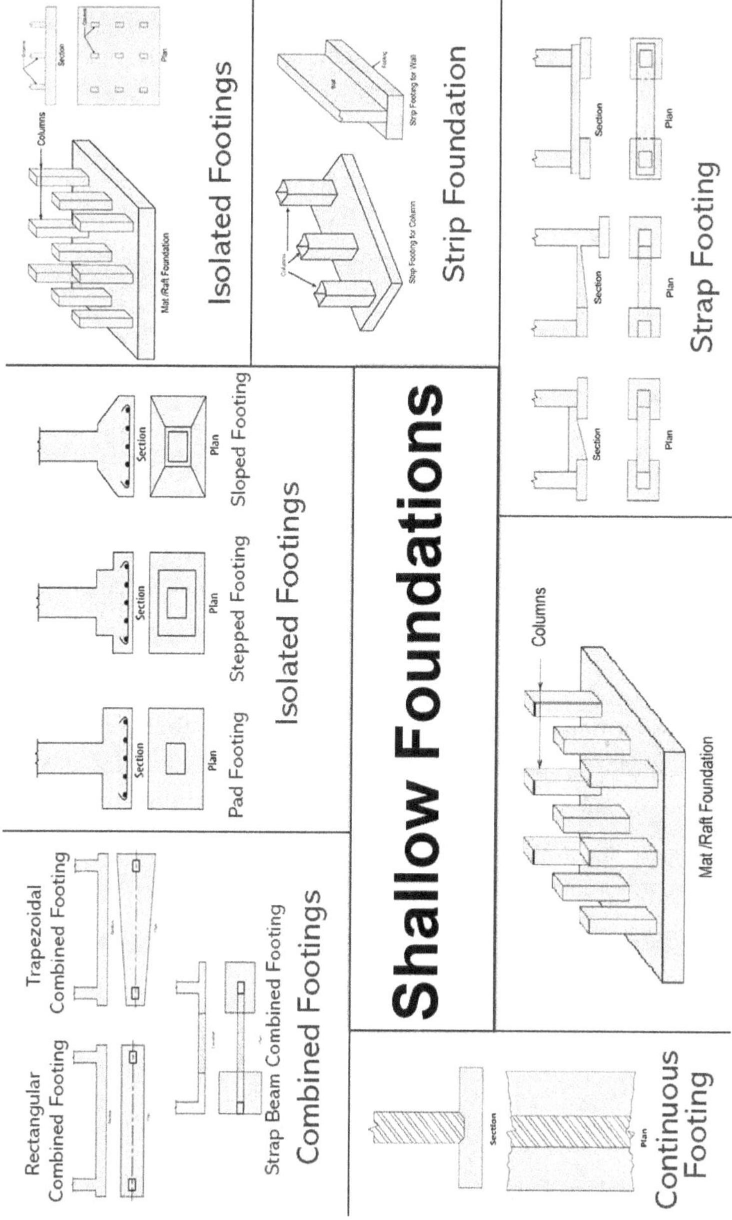

Fig. 4.2 Types of Shallow Foundation

There are a variety of shallow foundation types as shown in figure 4.2. These are some of the most prevalent types:

i.   **Strip footing:** When a load-bearing wall needs to be supported, it is placed on what are called "strip footings," which are long and narrow concrete pads. When the building's loads are uniformly distributed along the wall's length, shear walls are the preferred option. The weight that a strip footing can bear dictates how wide it needs to be.

ii. **Spread footing:** Individual columns or isolated loads are supported by spread footings. They are often wider than strip footings, and their shape is determined by the size and shape of the supporting column. They might be square, rectangular, or circular.

iii. **Mat foundation:** Mat foundations are often referred to as raft foundations. Many columns or walls are supported by these substantial, thick slabs of reinforced concrete. Mat footings are utilised when the building's loads are too heavy for strip or spread footings.

iv. **Combined footing:** When two or more columns are near together and their individual spread footings would overlap, combined footings are utilised. The purpose of combined footings is to transfer column loads evenly between them.

v.   **Strap footing:** When the columns are near together but not in a straight line, strap footings are utilised. A strap footing is comprised of two or more spread footings joined by a beam or strap.

vi. **Isolated footing:** Individual columns or small groups of columns are supported by individual footings. They are normally square or rectangular, and their size is determined by the load they will support.

In conclusion, shallow foundations are a frequent sort of support for constructions. The type of shallow foundation utilised is determined by the size and shape of the building, the loads it will hold, and the surface soil qualities.

Deep foundation: Deep foundation refers to a type of foundation that is used when the upper layers of soil are not capable of supporting the weight of the structure as shown in figure 4.1. In such cases, deep foundation techniques are employed to transfer the load of the structure to deeper, more stable layers of soil or rock. There are two main types of deep foundation: pile foundations and drilled shaft foundations.

i. **Pile Foundations:** When the soil at the surface cannot support the weight of the structure, pile foundations are employed. Long, slender structural pieces that are driven or drilled deeply into the earth are known as piles. Typically, they are made of steel, concrete, or wood. There are numerous varieties of pile foundations, such as:

- **End-Bearing Piles:** These piles distribute the structure's weight to a layer of rock or other hard material at the pile's base.

- **Friction Piles:** These piles rely on friction between the pile's surface and the surrounding soil to transfer the structure's weight.

- **Combination Piles:** These piles combine properties of end-bearing and friction piles.

ii. **Drilled Shaft Foundations:** When the soil or rock near the surface is too weak or unstable to support the structure's weight, drilled shaft foundations, also known as drilled piers or bored piles, are employed. A deep hole is drilled into the ground and then filled with concrete and/or reinforcing steel to form a sturdy, stable column. Two primary forms of drilled shaft foundations exist:

- **Auger cast Piles:** These piles are created by drilling a hole into the dirt and then slowly withdrawing the drill while filling the hole with concrete.

- **Caissons:** These are large, open-bottomed shafts that are generally used to support enormous constructions, such as bridges or skyscrapers. Typically, they are created underwater and then filled with concrete to make a sturdy base.

Generally, the choice of deep foundation type is influenced by a number of criteria, including as soil conditions, structural needs, and local construction standards and regulations. A competent engineer should be engaged in order to find the optimal deep foundation option for a specific project.

A structure's foundation is crucial because it provides the required support for the structure to stand safely and withstand the loads that it may be subjected to. The foundation serves several essential purposes, including supporting the structure's weight, distributing loads evenly, stabilising the structure, and preventing soil movement. To ensure the stability and lifespan of the project, it is essential to choose the proper type of foundation based on the soil conditions and the type of structure being constructed.

4.3 MASONRY WALLS

Masonry walls have been employed in building for millennia, and they remain popular today. A masonry wall is composed of bricks or stones that are held together with mortar. A masonry wall's aim is to provide structural support and act as a barrier to the elements. In this chapter, we will examine the many types of masonry walls, their benefits and drawbacks, and the criteria that should be considered when selecting masonry walls for a building project. Several types of masonry walls are available for use in building. They consist of:

- **Load-Bearing Masonry Walls:** To sustain the weight of the structure above them, load-bearing masonry walls are used as shown in figure 4.3(b). They are typically constructed from brick or concrete blocks and are meant to resist gravity and lateral loads. There are numerous methods for constructing load-bearing masonry walls, including solid masonry walls, hollow walls, and reinforced masonry walls.

- **Non-Load Bearing Masonry Walls:** Non-load-bearing masonry walls do not sustain the weight of the structure above them, but they nonetheless serve significant purposes, such as providing a barrier against the elements and insulation, as shown in figure 4.3(a). These walls are often constructed from lightweight materials like hollow concrete blocks or bricks and are not intended to sustain the same forces as load-bearing walls.

Masonry walls have a number of advantages and disadvantages that must be weighed prior to their selection for a construction project.

4.3.1 ADVANTAGES AND DISADVANTAGES OF MASONRY WALLS

Advantages:

i. **Durability:** With proper upkeep, masonry walls are extremely durable and can last for decades or even centuries.

ii. **Fire Resistance:** Masonry walls are highly fire-resistant and can prevent the spread of flames from one structure to another.

iii. **Sound Insulation:** Masonry walls provide exceptional sound insulation, which can be advantageous in noisy environments.

iv. **Thermal Insulation:** Masonry walls offer superior thermal insulation, which helps save energy expenses by keeping the building warm in the winter and cool in the summer.

v. **Low Maintenance:** Apart for the periodic repointing of mortar joints, masonry walls require minimal upkeep.

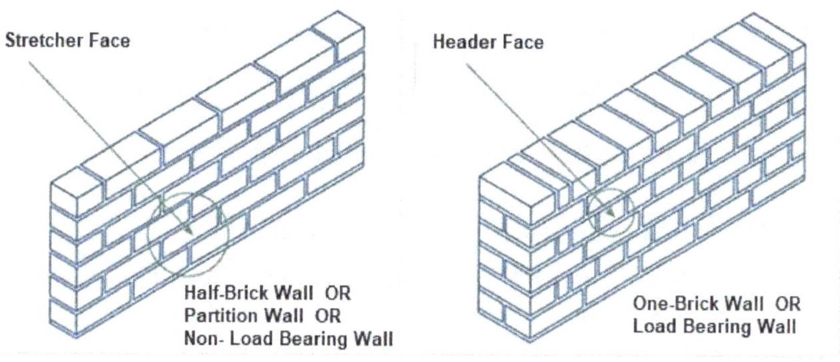

Fig. 4.3 a) Non-Load Bearing Walls or Partition Walls, b) Load Bearing Walls

Disadvantages:

i. **Cost:** Masonry walls are typically more expensive to construct than wood or metal walls.

ii. **Weight:** The weight of masonry walls is high which can raise the cost of the foundation and necessitate additional structural support.

iii. **Time-Consuming:** Masonry walls are typically more time-consuming to build than other forms of walls, which can raise construction costs and duration.

iv. **Limited Design Options:** Masonry walls provide restricted design alternatives, which might be disadvantageous for architects and designers that desire greater design flexibility.

4.4 COLUMNS

Columns are vertical structural elements used to support the weight of beams, slabs, and other elements above them. Columns come in a variety of shapes, sizes, and materials, and their design is determined by the need of the building or structure. Based on their ratio of slenderness, columns can be categorised as long or short. A long column is one in which the slenderness ratio is more than a given threshold, whereas a short column is one in which the slenderness ratio is less than that threshold. This topic examines the behaviour of long and short columns under various loading conditions.

i. **Long Columns:** A long column is one in which the slenderness ratio exceeds a specified threshold, which is typically 12 for steel columns and 10 for concrete columns. The slenderness ratio is defined as the proportion of the column's effective length to its smallest radius of gyration. The effective length of the column is the distance between its zero-moment points, which varies depending on the sort of end conditions. The radius of gyration measures the distribution of the column's cross-sectional area around its centroid.

When a long column is subjected to an axial compressive load, it deforms perpendicular to its axis. The buckling load can be calculated using Euler's formula:

$$P_{cr} = \pi^2 \, EI \, / \, (Kl)^2$$

Where,

P_{cr} is the critical buckling load

E is the modulus of elasticity

I is the moment of inertia of the column cross-section

Kl is the effective length of the column

K is a column end condition dependent component

A long column can be stopped from collapsing by providing lateral support at regular intervals. The lateral support may be given through bracing or intermediate supports.

ii. **Short Columns:** A short column is one in which the slenderness ratio is less than a predetermined threshold, which is typically 12 for steel columns and 10 for concrete columns. When a short column is subjected to an axial compressive force, the material will fail and be crushed. The following formula determines the load-carrying capability of a short column:

$$P_n = \varphi\, A_g\, f_{ck}$$

Where,

P_n is the nominal axial compressive strength

φ is a factor that accounts for numerous aspects including material qualities, load type, and reliability

A_g is the gross cross-sectional area of the column

f_{ck} is the compressive strength of the material.

Several aspects must be addressed in the design of columns, including the material qualities, loads to which the column will be subjected, end conditions, and slenderness ratio. Because it impacts the critical buckling load, the slenderness ratio is particularly relevant for long columns. The above formula can be used to compute the load-bearing capacity of short columns, whose design is generally basic. However, the design of lengthy columns is more complex, and it is necessary that the column is not susceptible to buckling. This can be accomplished by supplying the column with sufficient lateral support.

In buildings and other structures, columns are crucial structural components. Based on their slenderness ratio, they can be classed as long or short columns. Long columns are susceptible to buckling, whereas small columns fail due to material crushing. The design of columns should consider a number of aspects, such as the material qualities, the loads to which the column will be subjected, the end conditions of the column, and the slenderness ratio. Long columns require lateral support to prevent buckling, but short columns can be built using a simple formula.

4.5 BEAMS

Beams are structural elements that are primarily intended to support bending stresses. They are widely employed in construction and engineering to support roofs, floors, bridges, and other buildings. Several types of beams can be distinguished by their shape, cross-sectional dimensions, material, and manner of support, among other characteristics. This chapter will provide an introduction to beams and their various types.

4.5.1 TYPES OF BEAMS

i) Based on Shape:

- Rectangular Beams: Often employed in construction, these beams have a rectangular cross-section.

- Circular Beams: These circular-sectioned beams are frequently utilised for purposes such as light poles and flagpoles.

- I-Beams: These I-shaped beams are utilised extensively in construction due to their high strength-to-weight ratio.

- T-Beams: These T-shaped beams are frequently utilised in the building of floor and roof slabs.

- L-Beams: These "L"-shaped beams are frequently used in construction to hold walls or offer additional support to columns.

ii) Based on Cross-Sectional Dimensions:

- Solid Beams: Often employed in construction, these beams have a solid cross-section.

- Hollow Beams: These hollow-sectioned beams are utilised in sectors where weight reduction is crucial, such as aerospace.

- Composite Beams: These beams are constructed from a variety of materials and are often utilised in construction projects requiring high strength and longevity.

iii) Based on Material:

- Timber Beams: These wooden beams are often employed in construction.

- Steel Beams: Due to their excellent strength and longevity, these steel beams are frequently employed in construction.

- Concrete Beams: Due to their ability to resist compression, these beams composed of concrete are extensively employed in construction.
- Aluminium Beams: These aluminium beams are utilised in sectors where weight reduction is crucial, such as the aerospace industry.

iv) Based on Type of Support:

- Cantilever Beams: These beams are utilised in applications such as balconies and are supported at one end as shown in figure 4.4.
- Simply Supported Beams: These beams are utilised in applications such as bridges and are supported at both ends as shown in figure 4.4.
- Overhanging Beams: Beams are having some overhanging length on one side or both sides, majorly used in bridges or flyovers as shown in figure 4.4.
- Continuous Beams: These beams are supported at more than two locations and are frequently employed for greater spans in construction as shown in figure 4.4.
- Fixed Beams: Beams are having fixed support on both ends, majorly used in construction to carry load from slab and transfer to column as shown in figure 4.4.

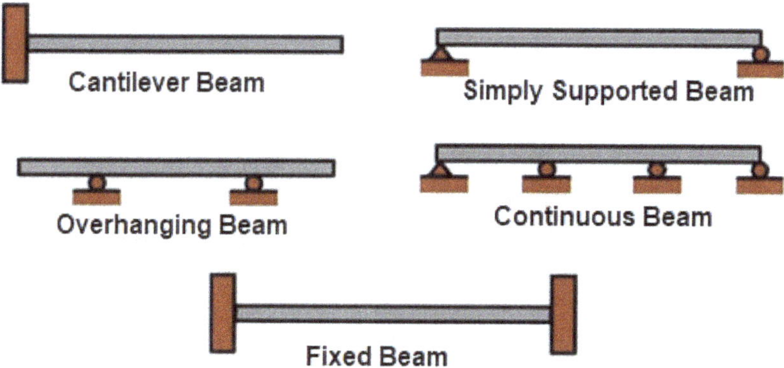

Fig. 4.4 Different Types of Beams as per End Supports

In conclusion, beams are a crucial element of construction and engineering, giving structural support and stability. There are numerous sorts of beams, each with their own distinct properties and purposes. Knowing the many types of beams and their qualities is essential for choosing the best appropriate beam for a specific application.

4.6 SLABS

Slabs are horizontal structural elements used to support building floors, roofs, and ceilings. There are several varieties of slabs used in construction, and each has its own pros and limitations. This chapter will explore the various slab kinds and their properties. Two typical types of reinforced concrete slabs differ in their capacity to resist bending in different directions: one-way slabs and two-way slabs.

- **One-Way Slab:** A one-way slab is a flat structural element that is designed to bear loads mostly in one direction and is supported by two opposing sides. In other words, the slab is intended to span in one direction alone, often from wall to wall. Reinforcing bars, commonly known as rebar, are positioned parallel to the slab's shorter span.

  The load on a one-way slab is transferred perpendicular to the span of the slab to the supporting beams or walls. One-way slabs are frequently utilized in residential and commercial structures, parking garages, and other structures where loads are predominantly concentrated in one direction.

- **Two-Way Slab:** A two-way slab is a flat structural element that is designed to carry loads in both directions and is supported on all four sides. The reinforcing bars are positioned in both directions perpendicular to one another, producing a grid-like design. The load on a two-way slab is transferred in both directions perpendicular to the span of the slab to the supporting beams or walls. Loads are typically distributed in various directions in bigger structures like as office buildings, retail malls, and airports, where two-way slabs are commonly employed.

One-way slabs are designed to predominantly resist loads in one direction, whereas two-way slabs are meant to withstand weights in two perpendicular directions. The choice of slab type will rely on the project's specific requirements, such as the size of the structure, the loads it will support, and the desired aesthetic and functional features.

Consult a structural engineer in order to establish which type of slab is acceptable for your project.

4.7 STAIRCASE

Staircases are one of the essential components of a building that provide vertical circulation between different levels. They have been around for centuries and have evolved with time, from simple steps cut into the rock to complex, curved, and decorative designs. Staircases not only serve a functional purpose but also add aesthetic value to a building. In this chapter, we will discuss staircases as a component of building, their types, design considerations, and construction.

4.7.1 TYPES OF STAIRCASES

There are numerous types of stairs that can be utilised in a structure, based on the available space, price, and design specifications. These are some of the most frequent staircase types:

i. **Straight Staircase:** The most prevalent type of stairway in structures is a straight staircase. It consists of a succession of ascending stairs with no landings or twists in between.

ii. **L-Shaped Staircase:** An L-shaped staircase consists of two straight flights of stairs linked by a landing that changes the stairs' orientation by ninety degrees.

iii. **U-Shaped Staircase:** A U-shaped staircase is composed of two parallel flights of stairs connected by a landing that changes the orientation of the stairs by 180 degrees.

iv. **Spiral Staircase:** A spiral staircase is a circular stairway that encircles a centre pole. It is typically utilised in small rooms or as a decorative element in buildings.

Constructing a staircase takes careful consideration of multiple issues, including available space, building laws, and safety regulations. Among the most significant design concerns for a staircase are:

i. **Rise and Run:** The rise is the height of each step, whereas the run represents its depth. The optimal ratio of rise to run is 1:2, or two inches of run for every inch of rise.

ii. **Headroom:** The minimum headroom required by building rules is 6 feet 8 inches, which is the vertical space above the stairs.

iii. **Tread and Riser Size:** The tread is the horizontal portion of a step that offers a walking surface, while the riser is the vertical component that links each tread. Ideal tread size is between 10 and 12 inches, and riser height should be uniform throughout the staircase.

iv. **Handrails and Balustrades:** The staircase's handrails and balustrades give support and safety. They must be robust, properly installed, and compliant with the local construction codes.

Staircases are an essential element of a building because they facilitate vertical circulation between levels. Their construction needs careful consideration of a number of criteria, including available space, building codes, and safety standards. A staircase that is well-designed and constructed not only serves a practical purpose but also adds aesthetic value to a building.

4.8 DOORS AND WINDOWS

Doors and windows are vital elements of both residential and commercial structures. They serve multiple functions, including as letting natural light and ventilation, giving access and security, and boosting the building's visual appeal. This chapter will provide an overview of the many types of regularly used doors and windows, their purposes, and the factors to consider when selecting them.

4.8.1 TYPES OF DOORS

i. **Hinged Doors:** Hinged doors are the most prevalent form of door in structures. They are hingedly attached to the frame and swing open and closed. Many materials, including wood, steel, and fibreglass, can be utilised to create hinged doors.

ii. **Sliding Doors:** Sliding doors consist of two or more panels that open and close by sliding along a track. They are frequently utilised in spaces with little space, such as closets, bathrooms, and patios.

iii. **French Doors:** French doors are a type of hinged door with two outward-opening doors. They are frequently utilised as patio, balcony, and garden entrances.

iv. **Pocket Doors:** With their ability to slide into a wall cavity, pocket doors are a good solution for regions with limited space. Often found in bathrooms and closets.

4.8.2 TYPES OF WINDOWS

i. **Casement Windows:** Casement windows have side hinges and open outward. They offer superior ventilation and are simple to clean.

ii. **Double-Hung Windows:** Double-hung windows consist of two vertically sliding sashes. They are simple to use and provide adequate ventilation.

iii. **Sliding Windows:** Sliding windows are an ideal alternative for spaces with limited space because they slide horizontally. They offer enough airflow and are simple to clean.

iv. **Bay Windows:** Bay windows consist of three or more windows that protrude from the building. They provide added interior space and an unimpeded view of the exterior.

4.8.3 CONSIDERATIONS FOR DOOR AND WINDOW SELECTION

- **Energy Efficiency:** By minimising heat loss and gain, energy-efficient doors and windows can aid in lowering energy costs. Consider purchasing doors and windows with a low U-factor and a high R-value.

- **Security:** Doors and windows should be constructed to give adequate protection from intrusion. Consider utilizing laminated or tempered glass, doors with a sturdy core, and high-quality locking mechanisms.

- **Aesthetics:** Doors and windows can dramatically affect a building's appearance. Consider the style and materials that complement the design and architecture of the building the most.

- **Maintenance:** Doors and windows must be regularly maintained to preserve their durability. Examine the maintenance requirements for different materials, such as wood, vinyl, and aluminium.

Doors and windows are essential to the operation, safety, and aesthetic appeal of any structure. There are numerous varieties of doors and windows available, each with its own distinct characteristics and advantages. Consider issues such as energy efficiency, security, aesthetics, and maintenance requirements when picking doors and windows. You can select doors and windows that increase the building's comfort and liveability with careful study.

4.9 JOINTS/CONNECTIONS

Joints or connectors are the points in a structure where two or more structural members meet. These connections are essential to the overall performance and stability of the structure. The ability of a structure to endure forces and loads is determined by the connections' strength and durability.

i. **Beam-Column Joint:** A beam-column joint is a critical connection point in a structural system where a beam and a column meet as shown in figure 4.5(a & b). The joint must be designed to transfer forces between the beam and the column, while also accommodating the movement and deformation of the structural members. There are different types of beam-column joints, including welded, bolted, and pinned connections. The design of the joint depends on factors such as the magnitude and direction of the forces acting on the joint, the size and shape of the structural members, and the material properties of the materials used.

Some common design considerations for beam-column joints include the use of adequate reinforcement, ensuring proper alignment and spacing of the reinforcement, and providing adequate shear transfer capacity. The joint must also be designed to resist bending moments, shear forces, and axial forces that are transferred between the beam and the column. The design of a beam-column joint is crucial to ensure the safety and stability of a building or structure. A poorly designed joint can lead to structural failure or collapse, which can have catastrophic consequences. Therefore, it is important to follow the applicable building codes and standards and seek the guidance of a qualified structural engineer during the design process.

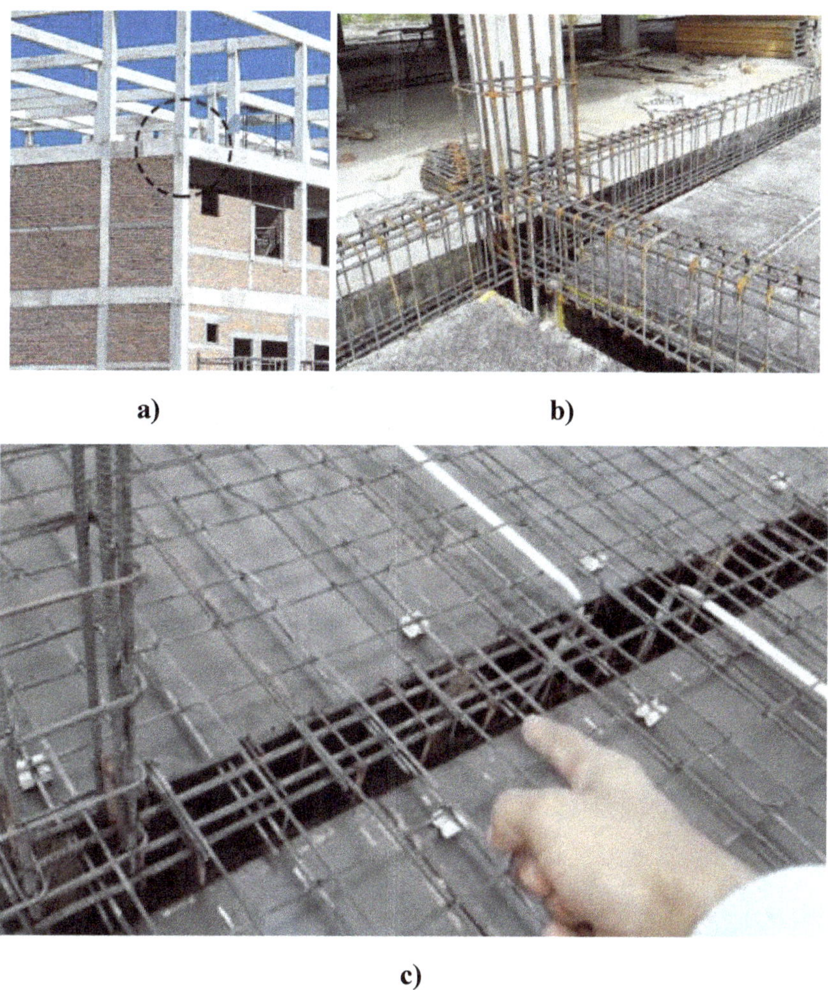

a)   b)

c)

Fig. 4.5 a) Beam-Column Joint, b) Reinforcement in Beam-Column Joint, and c) Beam-Slab Joint

ii. **Beam-Slab Joint:** A beam-slab joint is a connection between a reinforced concrete beam and a reinforced concrete slab in a building or structure as shown in figure 4.5(c). The joint must be designed to transfer the loads from the slab to the beam, while also accommodating the movement and deformation of the structural members.

The design of the beam-slab joint depends on factors such as the magnitude and direction of the loads acting on the joint, the size and shape of the beam and slab, and the material properties of the materials used. There are several types of beam-slab joints, including T-joints, L-joints, and rectangular joints.

In addition to structural design considerations, beam-slab joints must also be designed to prevent water leakage through the joint. This is typically achieved by using an appropriate joint sealant or by designing the joint with a small gap that can be filled with a flexible material.

There are also some other type of joints which considered very crucial zone of the structure such as column-footing joint, which needs proper design of the connection providing appropriate reinforcement. This contribution is majorly giving suggestions on beam-column joint as when this fails under any type of load, the complete structure falls down, so here will discuss how to avoid such things and if some kinds of cracks occur then how to cure such cracks and how to provide strength back to the joint. Detail discussion regarding the same with some design parameters will discuss in upcoming chapters.

OBJECTIVES AND MOTIVATIONS

5.1 GENERAL

Prior to 1970's, most of the reinforced concrete structures or buildings constructed with poor detailing of steel reinforcement at the joint locations due to the absence of design code requirements. The result of this poor detailing of steel reinforcement came as weakened link between beam and column which was the major reason of collapse of entire structure during seismic activities even moderate as seen in recent earthquakes as shown in figure 5.1 and 5.2, because beam-column joint is the crucial and critical region of any structure.

So, to reduce this damages and loss of lives during seismic action several research studies are giving their intensions on it and focusing to increase the shear and bond strength of beam-column joints. Most of the researches still are going in same direction as presented to strengthen the beam-column joint and most of the strengthening schemes have been developed and some of that can't be possible to apply practically due to their non-neglect able limitations, while strengthening the joint by using FRP composites is still in its early stage and many research efforts are focusing in this direction to develop applicable and reliable scheme.

5.2 OBJECTIVES OF THIS WORK

This investigation is to study the seismic retrofitting or rehabilitation of beam-column joint with corbel tested under monotonic loading using AFRP (Aramid Fiber Reinforced Polymer) so that joints of structures which constructed without consideration of seismic forces or seismic design and can't be able to resist seismic forces, can be retrofit and rehabilitate easily in future because reconstructing and demolishing the RC buildings are too expensive.

5.3 SCOPE OF THIS WORK

The experimental conclusions of this work will embolden future investigations in same direction for long term performance to enhancing this AFRP in structural applications where reconstructing and demolishing of RC buildings are difficult and expensive there retrofitting the limited fraction of structural components and building can offer a workable solution for ensuring the safety of structure and people.

Fig. 5.1 Damage Entire Structure due to failure action of Beam-Column Joint

Fig. 5.2 Damage of Beam-Column Joint under Seismic Action

6

Literature Study

6.1 GENERAL

Present part of this thesis presents a comprehensive up-to-date-literature review or prerequisite points allocated by previous researches in same direction on the upgrading of scarcity reinforced concrete beam-column joints, which vindicated to achieve aim of this study with advance composite materials. This chapter also presents performance as well as benefits and limitations of each rehabilitation scheme developed by some previous investigations on beam-column joint which are as:

[1]Fujii and Morita (2005) studied on experimental work to examine the shear strength of beam-column joint by the effect of shear reinforcement ratio and made a report that at 0.5% of shear strain there is degradation of joint shear rigidity under reversible load, and at shear strain of 1.5% and 2.8% both the joints exterior and interior attained on ultimate shear strength respectively.

[2]Aziz, and Biddah (2008) conducted experimental study on strengthening of exterior beam-column joint by using ductile material and found a excellent technique of strengthening as corrugated steel jacket around the column of exterior beam column joint. In this study, they tried double steel plates which bolted to the beam and joint, to cessation pull-out the bottom bars of the beam as shown in figure 3.1 and, found increment of 38% in strength and 180% in energy dissipation.

[3]Park and Tanaka (2011) have been studied the seismic behaviour on exterior and interior beam-column joints with substandard reinforcing. In this work, they developed a curve which describing the relationship of joint shear strength ratio and displacement ductility factor, and the curve representing increases the ductility of joint will increase shear strength of same joint.

[4]Corazao et al. (2000) has been experimental studied on interior and exterior joint by using epoxy bond external angles and plates to column face. In this study, it found that the interior and exterior strength was steepened by 21% and 18% respectively for retrofitted beam-column joint, and described a conclusion that the techniques which used in this study have shown to be excellent in restoring the capacity of joint with substandard reinforcement details.

[5]El-Amoury and Ghobarah (2010) proposed a series of repair schemes to enhance the joint shear strength and structural ductility by using CFRP composite as shown in figure 6.2 and it showed that imprisonment of the joint panel has ameliorate the ductility of structure and moment capacity of joint.

[6]Ghobarah and Said (2012) studied the rehabilitation schemes to the joint panel by various FRP composite and proposed the delaying of brittle shear mode of failure and the increment in shear resistance, and also represented improvement of performance, strength and ductility intimated by the hysteretic loops when compared to the control specimen.

[7] Clyde and Pantelides (2002) investigated experimental work using carbon fibre reinforced polymer composite laminates on one-way exterior joint and the corresponding results intimated the shear failure of joint in control specimens has shifted to the beam-column interface by using CFRP composites, and increment in the joint shear strength, maximum drift and energy dissipation capacity of rehabilitated samples found to be 5%, 78% and 200% respectively.

[8] Al-Salloum and Almusallam (2011) studied an experimental investigation of interior RC beam-column joints by using carbon fibre reinforced polymer composite laminates for the seismic response and corresponding results indicates the shear strength and ductility of beam-column joint enhanced with externally bonded carbon FRP, and also proposed this rehabilitate scheme vindicated the joint more stiffer against distortion.

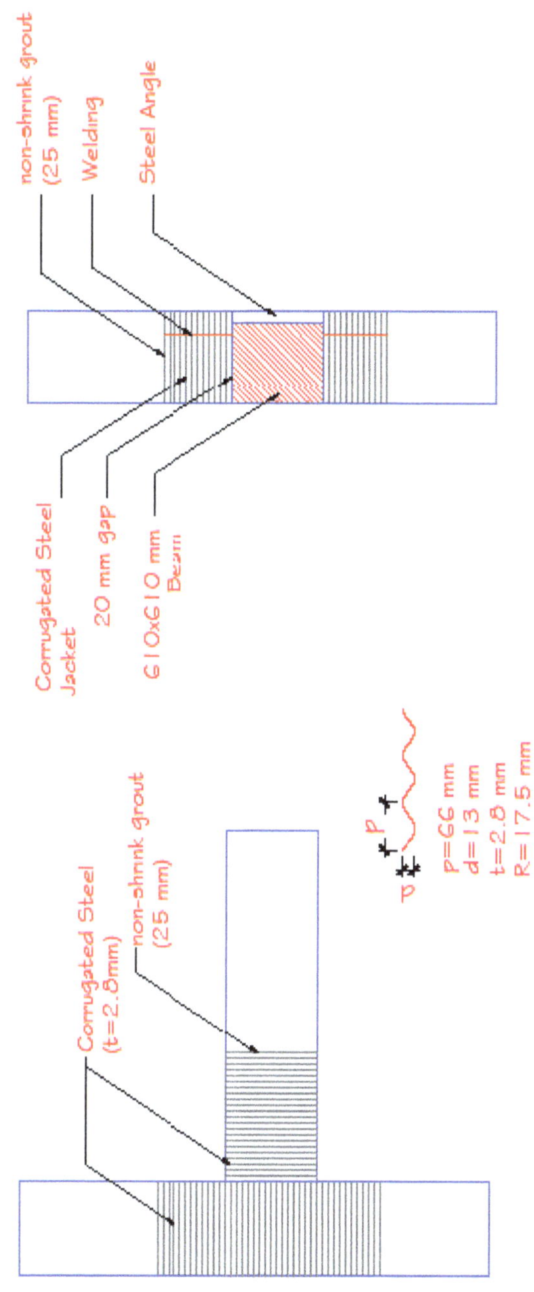

Fig. 6.1 Corrugated Steel Jacketing on Beam-Column Joint

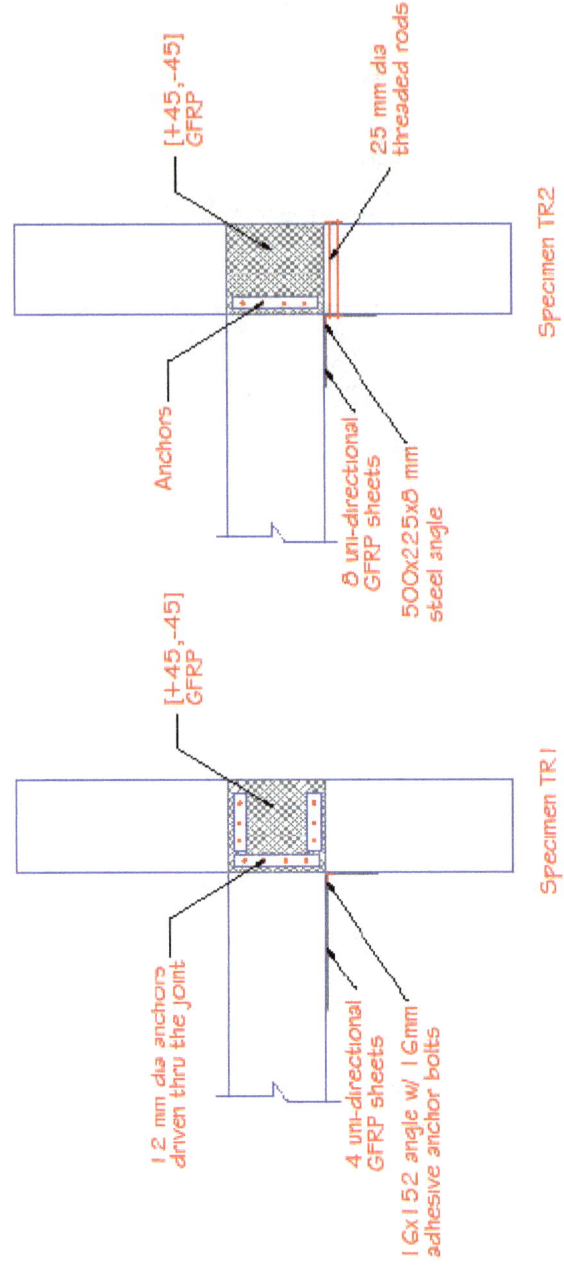

Fig. 6.2 CFRP Strengthening Technique

[9]Danesh and Alam (2013) conducted the experimental investigation to strengthening the corner beam-column joint by using GFRP composites and related findings indicates the excellent increment in ultimate load of 54% on rehabilitated specimen when it compared with control, and also intimates the improvement in shear strength and stiffness of the joint. It is also proposed that increment in load carrying capacity, reduction in story drift and changing the shear failure mode. The results of the research shows the effectiveness of the proposed rehabilitated GFRP techniques in increasing stiffness and shear strength of the joint, reducing story drift, increasing ultimate carrying capacity and changing the shear failure mode.

6.2 STRENGTHENING THE BEAM-COLUMN JOINTS

A variety of ways to strengthen the beam-column joint have been developed and introduced in past few years such as RC jacketing, steel jacketing, FRP composites etc, and some important and useful points which could be helpful to present study are as follows:

6.2.1 CONCRETE JACKETING

[10]Jirsa and Alcocer (2003) conducted experiential study on strengthen the beam-column joint by using concrete jacketing, it involves encasing the joint area as well as beam and column with extra longitudinal or transverse reinforcement which requires slab opening at the corner of column as shown in figure 6.3.

Hence, corresponding results found as beam was failed when jacketing wasn't used on it and also proposed 4% drift by steel cage and corner ties which confined joint satisfactory.

[11]Shannag and Alhassan (2005) studied experimental investigated to strengthening the beam-column joint by using 25 mm high performance fibre reinforced concrete jacketing with steel fibres all around the joint-column region. After detailed investigation, related findings intimates the improvement of rehabilitated samples in seismic behaviour and achieved some related parameters such as larger displacement, slower stiffness degradation, higher load levels and also higher energy dissipation, and it also proposed increment in column axial load and increased load carrying capacity of joint. But there is also a major

limitation of using concrete jacketing which is increment in dead load and size of member of the structure, and also poor appearance.

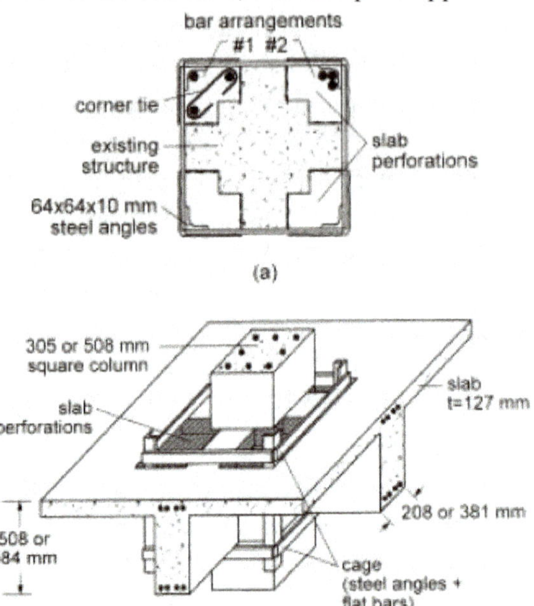

Fig. 6.3 Concrete Jacketing Technique

Fig. 6.4 Steel Jacketing Technique

6.2.2 STEEL JACKETING

Steel jacketing is the process of attaching the steel plates on joint face in all directions to enhance the shear strength and load bearing capacity of joint under seismic action and can use it in various shapes according to need as shown in figure 6.4. Non-shrink cement fills inside the gap between steel parts and joint region as grouting and for improvement in joint confinement steel parts are mechanically anchored with concrete, and bolts or adhesives are mainly used to make a strong bond between concrete surface and steel plates.

[12]Beres et al. (2012) conducted experimental study by using steel components with discontinuous bottom beam reinforcement to strengthen the interior as well as exterior beam-column joint where steel channels were bolted to make a proper bond between beam and column, and corresponding findings interior and exterior joint are found to be increment of 20% in peak strength & 10 to 20% in stiffness and increment of 33% in peak strength % 12% in stiffness, respectively.

[13]Ghobarah et al. (2016) conducted experimental study to strengthen the beam-column joint by using the steel jacketing with the help of bolts where cement grouting used to fill the gap portion between steel jacketing and joint surface, and related results proposed that increment in shear strength of rehabilitated joint and secondly, conversion of failure mode from flexural hinging in the beam.

6.2.3 FIBRE REINFORCED POLYMER COMPOSITES

[14]Arul (2016) conducted experimental study to strengthen the RCC beam-column joint by using carbon fibre reinforced polymer (CFRP) where corresponding results found as initial cracking load on rehabilitated specimen was increased more than 9% due to CFRP and failure would be at column in control & would be at beam in rehabilitated specimens.

[15]Pantelides and Okahashi (2008) conducted experimental investigation on Seismic Rehabilitation of RC Frame Beam-column Joint with FRP Composites and proposed results in which FRP helps to convert concrete from brittle manner to ductile manner and failure of joint under monotonic loading occurred at higher drift ratios.

[16]Hasan (2015) conducted experimental investigation on Seismic Strengthening of Reinforced Concrete Buildings by using FRP composite and proposed results in which the overall performance of the retrofitted beam-column joint had increased due to FRP Composites when compared to the control Specimens and FRP helps to convert concrete from brittle manner to ductile manner.

[17]Ramakrishna (2012) conducted experimental investigation on Rehabilitation of RCC Beam-Column Joints using glass fibre reinforced polymer (GFRP) Sheets and proposed some results in which it shows that tests on rehabilitated specimens suggest that FRP not only restore its original strength but also considerable enhancement in its yield load and initial stiffness.

6.3 FORCES ACTING ON BEAM COLUMN JOINT

The system of forces acting on beam-column joint depends on the type of joint and type of material used in it, and also type of load acting. There are three types of joints which interior, exterior and corner joints are discussed to examine effect of different loads with respect to different stresses which developed in them.

[18]Uma and Prasad (2013) conducted experimental investigation on seismic behaviour of beam column joints in reinforced concrete moment resisting frames. The forces subjected to gravity load on an interior joint as shown in figure 6.5(a), can be illustrated and some stresses can be transmitted directly through the joint which are tension and compression from the beam ends and axial loads from the column member, similarly when lateral loading or seismic action acts, due to this action produced forces from beam and column (which as shown in figure 6.5(b)) evolve diagonal tension and compression stresses within joint. Where cracks produced in joint are perpendicular to the tension diagonal *A-B* and produced at the joint face. There is no doubt about concrete which is weak in tension so to resist the diagonal tensile forces transverse reinforcement are used in that manner so that reinforcement can cross the plane of failure.

Now consider exterior joint and the forces acting on it can be intimated by figure 6.6, and shear force on it, is the only reason of diagonal cracks thus necessity of shear reinforcement is more in joint to prevent it from fail. Some of the reinforcement detailing expressed in figure 6.6(b) and 6.6(c) but longitudinal detailing of reinforcements affects significantly on efficiency of joint where 25-40% efficiency provided by bent up bars which laid away from joint and 85-100% efficiency given by anchored bars which laid in joint. However, shear reinforcement has to provide within the beam-column joint to confine concrete core.

Third one is corner beam-column joint and forces acting above it with continuous column shown in figure 6.7, can be perceived in similar way as that in an exterior beam-column joint w.r.t direction of loading. Some another type of corner joints such as wall type where moment is given either to close corner or open corner joint, and those joints also called as L-joints or knee joints and crack propagation of such joints is shown in figure 6.7.

The forces produced in opening joints and closing joints are exactly opposite with each other and the heavy cracks are oriented or intent along the corner diagonal where these type of joints proposed sufficient efficiency as compared to opening joints

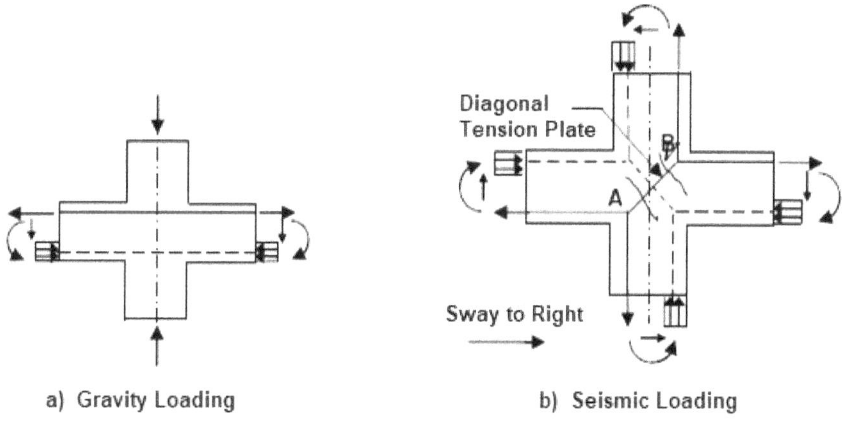

a) Gravity Loading

b) Seismic Loading

Fig 6.5 Gravity Action and Seismic Action on Interior Beam-Column Joint

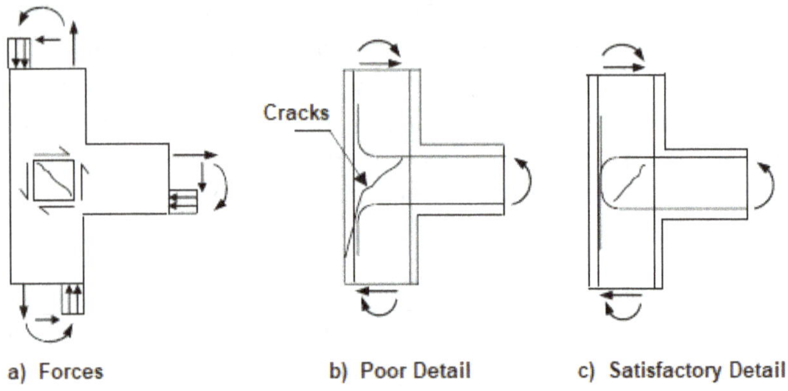

Fig. 6.6 Forces acting on Exterior Beam-Column Joint

6.4 JOINT MECHANISMS

[19]Meher and Umesh (2014) conducted experimental investigation on seismic behaviour of beam column joints in reinforced concrete moment resisting frames and reached on some points which are going to discuss now. At the ends, beams must be form plastic hinges and also produce extra flexural strength beyond design recommendations, where plastic hinges resist high internal forces because of crucial bond conditions of longitudinal steel which is passing from the joint region and also inflict high shear demand, and a complex interaction between shear and bond strength demonstration by behaviour of joint. Shear resisting mechanism to a significant extent affects by bond performance of the reinforcement bars which anchored in a joint

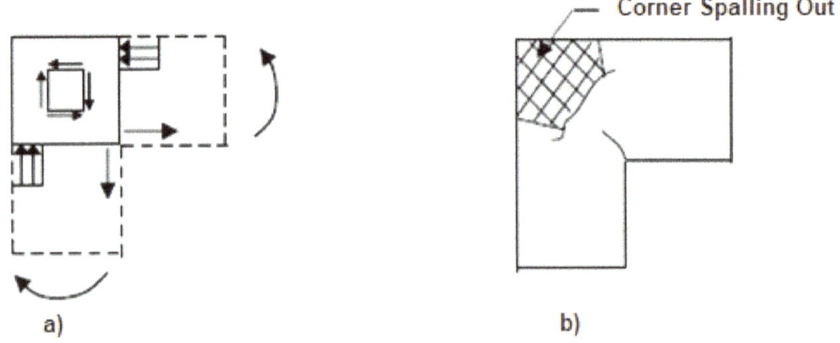

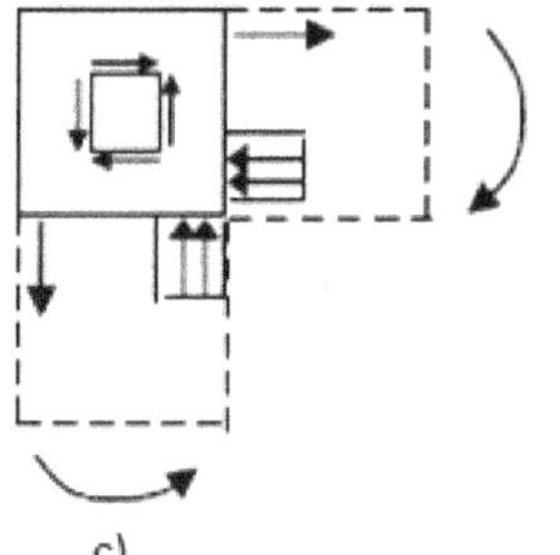

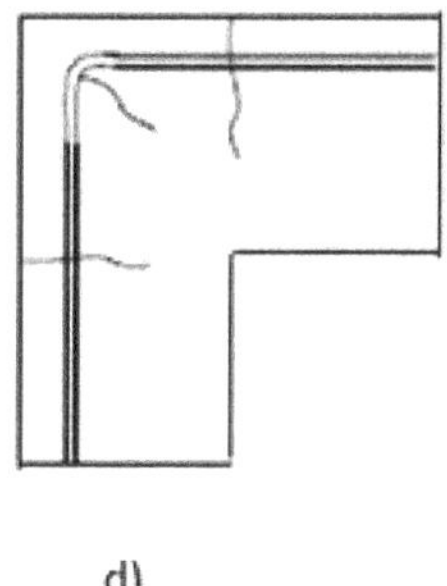

Fig. 6.7(a or c) Forces Acting on Corner Beam-Column Joint
Fig. 6.7(b or d) Crack Propagation of Corner Beam-Column Joint

6.5 BOND REQUIREMENTS

The forces tension or compression developed in the longitudinal reinforcements which passes through the beam-column joint, due to the reason of flexural forces produced in the beams and columns. Relatively huge tensile forces are transferred through bond during formation of plastic hinge. The term 'yield penetration' is referred as the formation of cracks introduced itself at the joint face along the bar when the longitudinal steel is stressed beyond yield splitting at the joint face. Enough and sufficient development length is to be ensured to taking yield penetration for the longitudinal steel within the joint into consideration, so requirements of bond have straight implication on sizes of RC framed beam-column joints.

6.5.1 FOR INTERIOR JOINTS

[21]Sayid and Ahmed (2011) conducted experimental investigation on behaviour of interior RC framed beam-column joint under action of load and proposed that the force in a bar changes from compression to tension which passes continuously through the joint, this process of conversion of force causes a effect of push-pull which obligate sufficient development length and imposes huge demand on bonding capacity or bond strength within the joint and it has to propitiate the necessities of tension and for compression force in same bar where figure 6.8 is expressing the distribution of bond along the longitudinal steel. The distribution of splitting cracks and inadequate development length into the joint core may result in slippage of steel bars in the joint. If the

limiting bond stress within the available development length, is exceeded only then can say occurrence of bar slippage. After detailed investigation by this author, it found that depth of column should be around 28 times the steel bar diameter to avoid bond deterioration only in case when development length is greater than 28 times of diameter of steel bar and concluded, there should be adoption of relatively smaller diameter bars so that column depth can also obtain smaller.

6.5.2 FOR EXTERIOR JOINTS

[21] Subramanian and Rao (2011) conducted experimental study on seismic design of exterior joint in RC framed structure and proposed the bond deterioration occurred at the face of column towards the joint core because of splitting cracks and yield penetration after a few cycles of inelastic loading. Repetition of loading increased the situation and maximum loss of bond on entire portion of bent bar may take place, and due to loss of bond longitudinal steel bars will get pulled-out or in simple words failure due to pull-out action of steel bars of beam is not completely unacceptable at any stage so accurate detailing and anchorage of longitudinal steel bars is most exigent or prerequisite. This type of major failure of bars in joint core region can be hold up and cessation by some positive anchorage or by provision of hooks as shown in figure 6.9, these hooks are advantageous to conferring adequate anchorage.

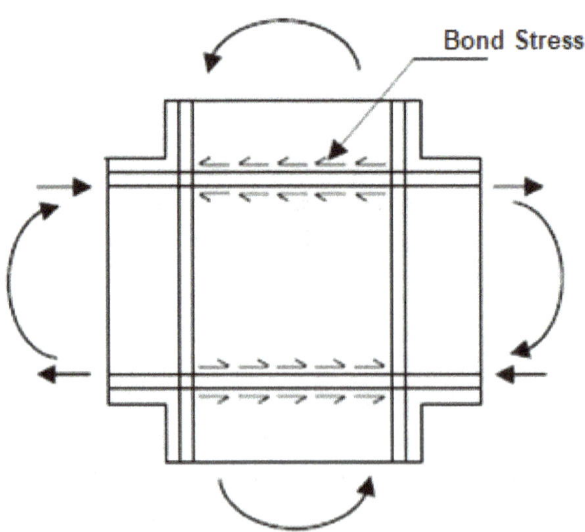

Fig 6.8 Bond Stresses in Interior Beam-Column Joint

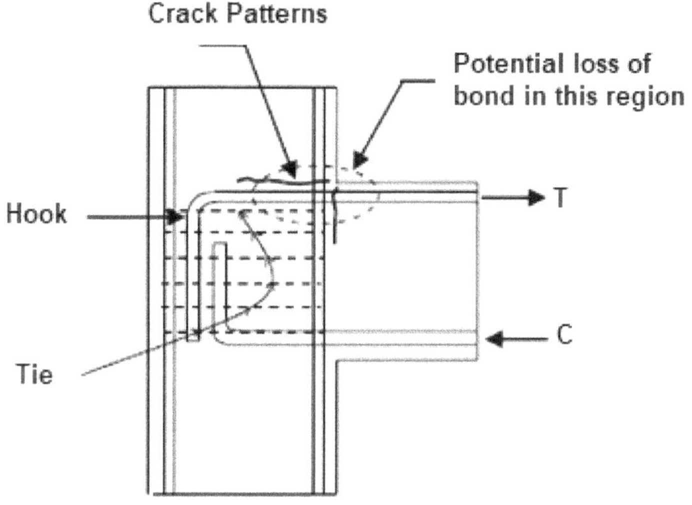

Fig 6.9 Formation of Hook in Exterior Beam-Column Joint

6.5.3 FOR CORNER JOINTS

[22] Kong and Bennison (2010) conducted experimental investigation on corner beam-column joint reinforcement details in RC framed structure with high strength concrete and corresponding findings which are bond requirement of longitudinal steel bars of corner beam-column joint core will be similar with same of exterior beam-column joint core because no specific code is there for bond requirement of corner or knee joints so reinforcement is provided to prevent shear failure so that beam displacement can increase prior to beam flexural yielding. The major disadvantage of the knee joints is retrofitting of bond deterioration is difficult as compared other joints.

7

DESIGN PROCESS

7.1 GENERAL

This chapter integuments comprehensively the detail description or exegesis regarding the design procedure of beam-column joint as per Indian Standard 456:2000 by limit state method, with suitable and required reinforcement steel bars, sizes of specimens, and also includes mix design proportion of different materials as per Indian Standard 10262:2009. The design guidelines of beam-column joint given by IS Code 456:2000 which follows limit state method to provide adequate strength and stiffness to joint so that it can resist un-wanted external forces formed from seismic and other un-required actions.

7.2 DESIGN OF BEAM-COLUMN JOINT

Beam-Column Joint is the crucial as well as critical zone in a reinforced concrete moment resisting frame. It is subjected to large forces during seismic activity or severe ground shaking and its performance has a significant influence on the response of the building. The functional requirement of a joint, which is the zone of intersection of beams and columns, is to enable the adjoining members to develop and sustain their ultimate capacity so as per its importance as structural component in any structure it designed as per Indian Standard 456: 2000 and 13920: 1993, which are as follows-

Design load & factored moment

Total Load (W)	= 5 kN/m
Factored Load (Wu)	= 10 kN/m
Design Moment (Mu)	= 0.553 kNm or 553161 Nmm
Req. Eff. Depth (Dreq)	= 40 mm
Lim. Moment of Resistance (Mu Lim)	= 1638821.8 Nmm

Adopt Section

Depth of Beam	= 100 mm
Clear Cover	= 20 mm
Dai of Stirrups & Main Bars	= 6 mm & 12 mm
Eff. Depth	= 68 mm
Eff. Length	= 875 mm

Reinforcement Design

Req. Area of Steel	= 157.7 mm^2
Prov. Area of steel	= 226.08 mm^2
Spacing	= 20mm

Shear Design

Nominal Shear Force	= 2.45 kN
Shear Stress	= 0.3615 N/mm^2
Max Shear Strength	= 3.5 N/mm^2
Design Shear Strength	= 0.77 N/mm^2
Spacing of stirrups	= 100 mm

Check

Moment of Resistance	= 2997770.583 N
Development Length	= 451.31 mm

Design summary

Cross-section $_B$	= 100 mm x 100 mm
Cross-section $_C$	= 100 mm x 100 mm
Length of column	= 1000 mm
Length of Beam	= 750 mm from edge of col.
Main Tensile bars$_B$	= 2-10 mm dia of Fe-415
Main Reinforcement $_C$	= 4-8 mm dia bars
Vertical ties	= 6 mm dia @ 75 mm c/c
Shear stirrups	= 6 mm dia of 2-legged
Anchor Bars	= 2-8 mm dia bars

7.3 PREPARATION OF MIX DESIGN

The process of selecting suitable ingredients or raw material of composite like concrete and determining or calculating of their relative amounts with the objective of producing a concrete in required strength, durability, and workability with as much as economically, is termed the concrete mix design. There are some guidelines to complete this design process in Indian Standard 10262:2009 by which it prepared and found materials with relative amount as shown in table 7.1.

7.3.1 FACTORS TO BE CONSIDERED FOR MIX DESIGN

Some factors which are required or compulsory to considered, are as follows:

a) The grade designation giving the characteristic strength requirement of concrete.

b) The type of cement influences the rate of development of compressive strength of concrete.

c) Maximum nominal size of aggregates to be used in concrete may be as large as possible within the limits prescribed by IS 456:2000.

d) The cement content is to be limited from shrinkage, cracking and creep.

e) The workability of concrete for satisfactory placing and compaction is related to the size and shape of section, quantity and spacing of reinforcement and technique used for transportation, placing and compaction.

7.3.2 DESIGN STIPULATIONS

- Characteristic Compressive Strength required after 28 days: 38.25 N/mm^2
- Maximum size of Aggregate: 20mm (Angular)
- Type of Cement: OPC 53 Grade
- Maximum Cement Content: 450kg/m^3
- Minimum Cement Content: 320kg/m^3
- Maximum Water Cement Ratio: 0.42
- Maximum Water Content: 186 lts (For 20mm Aggregates)

- Workability: 100mm
- Chemical admixture type: Super Plasticizers (Sp. Gravity = 1.145)
- Type of Exposure: Severe (For Reinf. Concrete)
- Method of Concrete Placing: Manually
- Method of Mixing: Machine
- Degree of Supervision: Good
- Degree of Quality Control: Good

7.3.3 MIX DESIGN DATA FOR M30 GRADE OF CONCRETE

Grade Designation	M30
Type of Cement Used	OPC 53 Grade
Nominal Max. size of Aggregate Used	20 mm
Admixtures	2% By Mass of Cement
Take Water Cement ratio	0.42
Specific Gravity of Cement	3.14
Specific Gravity of Coarse Aggregate	2.74
Specific Gravity of Fine Aggregate	2.63
Workability	100mm

7.3.4 DESIGN PROCEDURE

Target Mean Strength

$$Fck' = fck + 1.65S$$
$$= 30 + 1.65 * 5$$
$$= 38.25 N/mm^2$$

Fck' = Target mean compressive strength at 28days, in N/mm^2.

fck = Characteristic compressive strength at 28days, in N/mm^2.

S = Assumed Standard deviation N/mm^2. (Depends on grade of concrete)

Calculations of Cement Content:

- Water Cement Ratio = 0.42 [W/C = 0.42]
- Estimated Water Content = 186 + (186*6/100)

(For 75-100mm Slump) = 197 Lts

[W.C. + 3% of W.C. For each 25mm increased Slump as per Code]

As super plasticizer is used, the water content can be reduced up 20 percent and above. Based on trials with super plasticizer water content reduction of 29 percent has been achieved. Hence,

Arrived Water Content = 197 x 0.71

  = 140 ltr

- Req. Cement Content = 140/0.42

  (Per Meter Cube) = 333 kg

(Min. Cement Content < Req. Cement Content < Max. Cement Content)

- Volume of Coarse Aggregate = 0.62

(for Zone II *Table No.3 IS 10262 – 2009*)

- Volume of Fine Aggregate = 1 – 0.62 = 0.38

Mix Calculations:

Volume of Concrete $= 1 \text{ m}^3$

Volume of Cement $= \dfrac{Mass\ of\ Cement * 1}{Specific\ Gravity\ of\ Cement * 1000}$

  $= (333/ 3.14) * (1/1000) = 0.106 \text{ m}^3$

Volume of Water $= \dfrac{Mass\ of\ Water * 1}{Specific\ Gravity\ of\ Water * 1000}$

  $= (140/ 1.0) * (1/1000) = 0.140 \text{ m}^3$

Vol. of Chemical Admixtures $= \dfrac{Mass\ of\ Admixture * 1}{Specific\ Gravity\ of\ Admixture * 1000}$

  $= \dfrac{(333 \times 2 \div 100) \times 1}{1.145 \times 1000}$

  $= 0.0058 \text{ m}^3$

Note: Super Plasticizers @ 2% by Mass of Cementations Material

Volume of All Aggregates = 1 – [Vol. of Cem.+Vol. of Wat.+Vol of Adm.]

 = 1 - [0.106 + 0.140 + 0.0058]

 = 0.75 m^3

Mass of Coarse Aggregate = 0.75 * Vol. of CA *

(Per Meter Cube) Specific Gravity of CA * 1000

 = 0.75 * 0.62 * 2.74 * 1000

 = 1274 kg

20mm Aggregates = 0.62 * 1274 = 790 kg/m^3

12mm Aggregates = 0.38 * 1274 = 484 kg/m^3

Mass of Fine Aggregate = 0.75 * Vol. of FA *

(Per Meter Cube) Specific Gravity of FA * 1000

 = 0.75 * 0.38 * 2.63 * 1000

 = 750 kg

Mix Ratio **= 1 : 2.3 : 3.8**

Table 7.1 Concrete Mix Proportions

Concrete Mix Properties for 1 Cubic Meter				
Water kg/m^3	Cement kg/m^3	Fine Aggregate kg/m^3	Coarse Aggregate kg/m^3	
			12.5 mm	20 mm
140 kg/m^3	333 kg/m^3	750 kg/m^3	484	790
			1274 kg/m^3	
0.42	1	2.3	3.8	

7.4 DETAIL OF THE SPECIMENS

The dimensions and reinforcement detail of the beam-column joint used in present study are shown in figure, and beam-columns are as follows:

Design Load of Joint   = 10 kN

Req. Area of Steel   = 157.7 mm^2

Prov. Area of steel   = 226.08 mm^2

Beam

Cross section   = 100mm x 100mm with length 750mm.

Top Reinforcement   = Two bars of 8mm diameter.

Bottom Reinforcement   = Two bars of 10mm diameter and one bar of 8mm diameter.

Stirrups   = 6mm diameter with the spacing of 75mm centre to centre (c/c).

Column

Cross section   = 100mm x 100mm with length 1000mm.

Main Reinforcement   = Four bars of 8mm diameter.

Vertical Ties   = 6mm diameter with the spacing of 75mm centre to centre (c/c).

Cubical Specimens   = 100 mm x 100 mm x 100 mm

Prisms   = 100 mm x 100 mm x 500 mm

Cylindrical Specimen   = 100 mm x 200 m

8

Experiental Programme

8.1 GENERAL

This chapter integuments comprehensively the detail description or exegesis of the experimental programme, which comprises the description and designation of specimens and their corresponding materials which used as well as the proposed rehabilitation schemes by aramid fibre reinforced polymer (AFRP), the experimental set-up, instrumentation and investigation, and also the test procedure from beginning to end. It also includes different attributes of materials such as binding material, aggregates etc which found by preliminary laboratory tests such as specific gravity test, test by vicat apparatus, soundness test, bulking of sand test and many more, to find their behaviour w.r.t water, and also testing on concrete such as slump test etc comprised in this chapter. After preliminary finding on materials this chapter includes mix design proportions of materials to build concrete as per Indian Standard code 10262:2009 which helped to find standard proportion of materials by weight or by volume but in this investigation all materials quantities taken by as weight with standard water cement ratio throughout the project work. Next step is the casting of specimens which is completely depends on previous one which discussed above because through specimen design, can get actual quantity of concrete. After this soft work many steps are there such as casting of specimens which includes process of making the specimens of required sizes, curing of specimens in dust free water for 28-days of long period as per Indian Standards so that samples can achieve maximum strength as per design recommendations, testing on different specimens under monotonic load by universal testing machine to find their strength and other required properties such as stiffens, ductility ratio etc.

8.2 DIFFERENT MATERIALS AND THEIR PROPERTIES

Many of materials which are binding material such as Ordinary Portland Cement of 53-grade, different sizes of aggregates such as fine aggregates of size less than 4.75mm to fill voids, coarse aggregates of size 12.5mm and 20mm to provide strength, higher water reducer type super-plasticizer to control workability of concrete, epoxy materials such as Araldite GY 257 and Hardener HY 840 in ratio of 1:0.5 respectively and fresh water with dust free nature, and also aramid fibre reinforced polymer (AFRP) sheet which is a non-degradable substance has no melting point and has good resistance to abrasion, are used in this experimental work to prepare concrete and rehabilitate it, are as follows:

8.2.1 BINDING MATERIAL

Binding material or cement is used in present work of OPC 53-grade which is a great binder has excellent binding properties or in simple words it is a substance used in construction work which helps hardens and adheres to other materials and also binding them together. In concrete manufacturing process cement used to bind sand and gravel (aggregate) together. When cement is used with only fine aggregate it produced mortar, or with sand and gravel aggregates it produced concrete. Before use of it in this work, it tested by preliminary tests as shown in figures 8.1 & 8.2, to determine important properties such as soundness, initial and final setting time, consistency etc. So, the different attributes of cement as per Indian Standard 12269:1989 are shown in table 8.1.

8.2.2 AGGREGATES

Aggregates are the most useful and common materials for worldwide construction which occupies most of the volume of concrete, and are a major component of composite material which deputizes as reinforcement and provide strength to composite material like to concrete. Maximum Strength of concrete is depends on attributes and behaviour of aggregates such as shape of aggregates, particle size distribution inside wetness etc. Chemical reaction between dust free aggregates and cement paste creates bond or strength between them. So can say, aggregates are the major factor by which concrete gains its strength. The different important attributes of aggregates were determined by some preliminary tests as shown in figures 8.3 & 8.4, as per Indian Standard 2386:1963 as shown in table 8.2.

- **Coarse aggregates:** Coarse aggregates were use in this research work which was 20mm as well as 12.5mm size with free from dust and aggregates were crushed angular shape type, used to provide strength of concrete.

- **Fine aggregates:** Fine aggregates were use of less than 4.75mm size which means, are passing through 4.75mm sieve. It helps to fill voids in concrete mixture and assist in producing uniformity and workability.

8.2.3 ARAMID FIBRES

The aramid fibres are produced by spinning of dissolved polymer to a solid fibre from a liquid chemical blend and because of its high tensile strength-to-weight ratio by this measure these are 5 times stronger than steel. These types of fibres are currently three types which available in market such as Kevlar, Twaron and Technora by name of trade, and these are highly organic type fibres. These are the superstar family in fibre world which are a class of heat-resistant and strong synthetic fibre. The name of fibre comes from a combination of two words, "Aromatic Polyamide". These fibres have excellent attributes such as good resistance to abrasion, no melting point, low flammability, non-conductive, sensitive to ultraviolet radiations as well as acids and salts etc. Due to their superior strength-to-weight ratio and heat-resistant properties, aramid fibres can be used in retrofitting of structural components to improve their strength against seismic activities. Here, these fibres are used in retrofitting or rehabilitation of beam-column joint which is a crucial zone in structure.

Table 8.1 Properties of Cement

Property	Average value of OPC used in this investigation	Standard value
Specific Gravity	3.14	----
Consistency (%)	32	----
Initial setting time (min.)	74	>30

Final setting time (min.)	240	<600
Soundness	2.9	<10
Fineness	98.50	----

Table 8.2 Properties of Aggregates

Property	Fine Aggregates	Coarse Aggregates
Specific gravity	2.63	2.74
Water absorption	0.67	0.95
Size of Aggregates (mm)	< 4.75	< 20
Bulking of Sand (%)	28	----
Sieve Analysis	Zone III-confirming to IS 383:1970	----

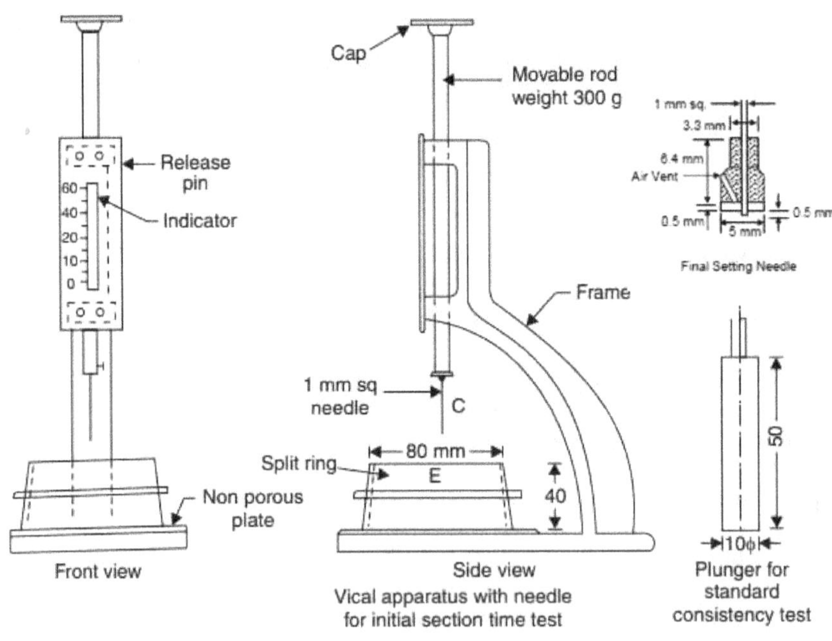

Fig 8.1 Vicat Apparatus to find Consistency and Setting time of Cement

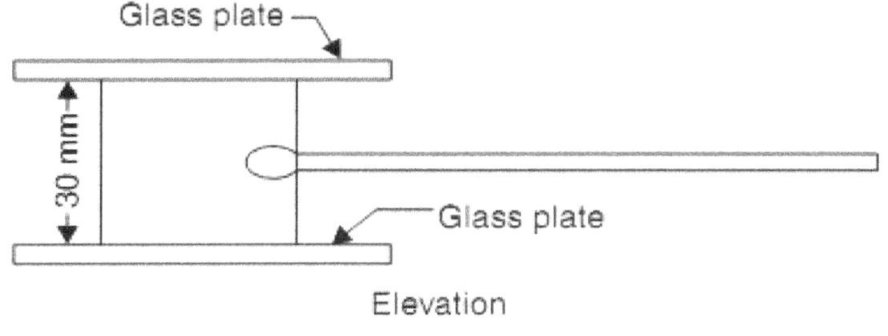

Fig 8.2 Le-Chatelier Apparatus to find Soundness of Cement

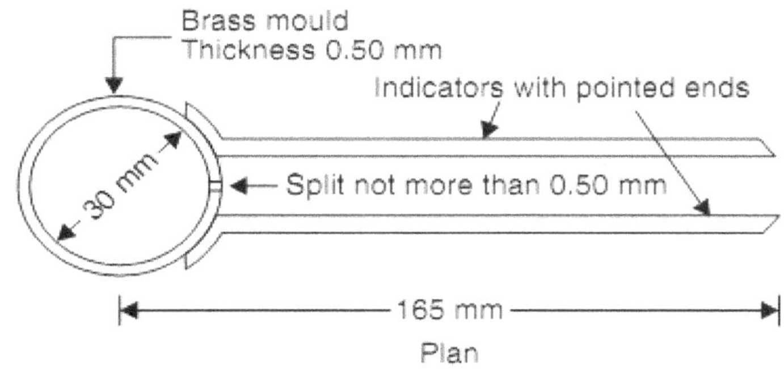

Fig 8.3 Fine Aggregates
(< 4.75mm)

Fig 8.4 Coarse Aggregates
(20mm)

8.3 PREPARATION OF SPECIMENS

In this experimental work, IS code 10262:2009 used for prepare M_{30} concrete mix by using OPC- 53 grade cement, fine aggregates which passed through 4.75mm sieve, dust free coarse aggregates of two different sizes (20mm and 12.5mm) of crushed angular shape, BASF types super-plasticizer or highly water reducer chemical, fresh water and with 0.42 standard water cement ratio. Standard dosage of super-plasticizer (0.6% of cement by weight) was used in this mix to maintain concrete workability. This concrete mix was moulded in form of standard 100mm x 100mm x 100mm size of cube mould, 100mm x 100mm x 500mm size of prisms, 100mm x 200mm size of cylinders and artificial mould of exterior beam-column joint where column size was 100mm x 100mm with height 1000mm and beams size was 100mm x 100mm with length 750mm, and inside surface of all the moulds were oiled properly so that they could be de-moulded easily without any damage of specimen.

Required quantities of given materials were mixed with accurate proportion in drum type mixing machine with proper batching, where batching is defined as "the process of measuring the materials and inosculate all the measuring material on one place in proper proportion".

Mixing was continued till uniform mixing of raw material, could be achieved. Once the raw materials were mixed completely, mixture was placed in bigger pan and then it poured in cube shaped moulds, prisms and cylinders for compressive strength test, flexural strength test and split tensile strength respectively and also in T-shaped moulds or exterior beam-column joint mould and vibrated it properly for sufficient time so as not to have any voids. Reinforcement steel bars of different diameter and numbers as per design parameters mentioned in chapter-7 were used in T-shaped moulds with proper spacing of stirrups. Inside portion of moulds were coated with oil before pouring concrete so that samples could be remove easily from moulds after 24 hours. Moulds were filled with mixture in three different layers and each layer was tamped 25 times with the help of steel tamping rod. After 24-hours, when mixture settled thoroughly in moulds, de-moulded it and kept for required period of wet curing as per Indian Standard guidelines, in dust free water curing tank. The whole process of preparation of specimens is shown in different figures 8.5 to 8.10.

Fig 8.5 Preparation of Cubical Mould

Fig 8.6 Prepared Prisms or Beams Specimens

Fig 8.7 Preparation of T-Shaped Moulds

Fig 8.8 Prepared T-Shaped Specimens

Fig 8.9 Pouring of Concrete in T-Shaped Mould

Fig 8.10 Curing of Different Specimens

8.4 INVESTIGATION ON MACHENICAL PROPERTIES

Compressive strength is defined as the capacity of a material or specimen or structure to withstand force tending to reduce size, as averse to tensile strength, which withstands forces tending to lengthen or deformed. In simple words, compressive strength resists compression (being pushed together), whereas tensile strength resists tension (being pulled apart). In the study of strength of materials, tensile strength, compressive strength, and shear strength can be analyzed independently.

Some materials can be fracture at their compressive strength limit; others deform irreversibly, so a given amount of deformation may be considered as the limit for compressive load so can say it is a key value for design of structures.

8.4.1 COMPRESSIVE STRENGTH

Compressive strength is nothing but a maximum applied load to the cross-sectional area of used sample. The ultimate compressive strength of a material or any specimen is the value of uni-axial compressive stress reached when the material fails completely under applied load. The compressive strength obtained usually experimentally by means of a compressive test under compressive load on cubical specimens by universal or compressive testing machine as shown in figure 8.11. Strength is always depends on type of material used in specimen which going to test, like compressive strength of concrete depends on its grade, higher the grade strength will be high. In present study, compressive strength found on cubical specimens of size 100 x 100 x 100 mm in control as well as by using aramid fibre reinforced polymer (AFRP) sheet by wrapping in three different layers on the surface of specimens in all directions with the help of epoxy resin which is nothing but a composite of Araldite GY 257 and Hardener HY 840 in proportion of 1:0.5 respectively. After testing of these specimens with or without AFRP sheet, test results were comprised with each other.

8.4.2 FLEXURAL STRENGTH

Flexural strength, also known as bend strength, or transverse rupture strength, or modulus of rupture, is an important attribute of material or any specimen, defined as the stress in a material or specimen just before it yields in a flexure test. The transverse bending test is most frequently employed, in which a specimen having either a circular or rectangular cross-section is bent until fracture or yielding using a third point flexural test technique as well as centre point technique. Strength is always depends on type of material used in specimen which going to test, like flexural strength of concrete depends on its grade, higher the grade strength will be high. In present study, flexural strength found by centre point loading system as shown in figure 8.12, on prisms or beams of size 100 x 100 x 500 mm in control as well as by using aramid fibre reinforced polymer (AFRP) sheet by wrapping in three different layers on the surface of specimens in all directions with the help of epoxy resin which is nothing but a composite of Araldite GY 257 and Hardener HY 840 in proportion of 1:0.5 respectively. After testing of these specimens with or without AFRP sheet, test results were comprised with each other.

Difference between Centre-Point loading and Third-point loading method

a) The major difference between both of them is location of load application. In ASTM C 293 method or centre-point loading, load acts at the centre of beam but opposite in ASTM C 78 method or third-point loading, position of load application is $1/3^{rd}$ of span from both supports.

b) In ASTM C 78 method, prism length is subjected to Maximum bending moment but in other method, only cross-section of sample at mid length is subjected to maximum bending moment.

c) The modulus of rupture (MR) determined by ASTM C 293 or centre-point loading is always greater than modulus of rupture (MR) determined by ASTM C 78 or third-point loading.

8.4.3 SPLIT TENSILE STRENGTH

Tensile testing is also named as tension testing, which is nothing but a fundamental materials science test in which specimen is subjected to a controlled tension until failure. The results from this test are commonly used to select a material for quality control, for an application, and to predict how a material will react under different types of loads. That attributes which are directly measured via tensile test, are maximum elongation, ultimate tensile strength, and reduction in area. From these finding, many attributes such as Young's modulus, Poisson's ratio, yield strength, and strain-hardening characteristics etc can also be determined. Strength is always depends on type of material used in specimen which going to test, like compressive strength of concrete depends on its grade, higher the grade strength will be high. In present study, split tensile strength found by transverse loading system as shown in figure 8.13, on cylindrical specimens of size 100 x 200 mm in control as well as by using aramid fibre reinforced polymer (AFRP) sheet by wrapping in three different layers on the surface of specimens in all directions with the help of epoxy resin which is nothing but a composite of Araldite GY 257 and Hardener HY 840 in proportion of 1:0.5 respectively. After testing of these specimens with or without AFRP sheet, test results were comprised with each other.

8.5 INVESTIGATION ON EXTERIOR BEAM-COLUMN JOINT

8.5.1 TEST DESCRIPTION

As mentioned earlier, the objective of present experimental work test is to study the behaviour of deficient non-seismically designed RC beam column joint under dynamic impulse load or monotonic loading so that after detailed investigation on it, that building which were constructed non-seismically and that which are damaging during earthquake or has been damaged, can be retrofit and rehabilitate economically and convert them seismic resistant buildings. Hence, beam-column joint specimens are designed non-seismically so that they can be tested as control and then by wrapping of AFRP sheet, and fail control samples can be rehabilitate with the help of AFRP sheet.

8.5.2 TEST SETUP AND LOADING CONDITIONS

The mechanisms of this test setup are designed to transfer the forces horizontally, vertically as well as laterally, generated under typical seismic actions where lateral loading could be possible, in cast-in-place reinforced concrete (RC) beam-column joint. The vertex of the joint's column is attached to an axial loading beam that spins with the joint specimen movement through a uni-directional hinge assembled between the axial steel rod and the strong floor. A lateral horizontal load is also enforced to the vertex of the column by calibrated actuator. The bottom base of the joint's column is supported on a steel hinge support that allows spinning of the column in the in-plane flank, while the end of the beams away from the joint is also pinned to assent the beam spinning at the inflection point.

The beam-column joint specimen was initially loaded at the starting of this experimental test, with axial load to determine the consequences of vertical gravity loading. Subsequent to enforcing the axial load on the column, the specimen was loaded with dynamic impulse loading due to sudden or unaware motion of the actuator at the starting of the test. The rapid motion of the actuator has exerted an impulse loading over small-time interval and it became the reason of rupture of the beam-column joint specimen. The impulse loading w.r.t time was recorded during the testing. The corresponding findings of the unaware dynamic loading enforced on the joint specimen was utilized to examine the behaviour of exterior beam-column joint considering the consequences of seismic loads at near faults.

After enforced of gravity loading only, now specimen was loaded with constant axial load as well as cyclic horizontal lateral load at the vertex of the column where prior to cyclic lateral load, axial load was enforced through hydraulic jacks on the vertex of the load transfer beam. Where, calibrated load cell is used to measure cyclic load which enforced by hydraulic actuator on vertex of the column. At every push and pull action of cyclic load until connection failure increment in displacement was increased.

8.5.3 TESTING DETAIL

The testing arrangement of beam-column joint is shown in tested which showed in figure 8.14, with a constant axial load on the column vertex and a static load at the beam tip. Beam-column joint was tested by hydraulic jacks under initial restraining force of 10kN to the column. The monotonic load test was conducted on the control and retrofitted specimens of reinforced concrete joint. If the column axial load applied by the hydraulic jacks, exceeded by one-half of its capacity, the effect of axial load will be more on the joint.

So as to maintain the seismic load or earthquake load behaviour on beam-column joint, the axial load was controlled and it is decided to apply the load up to one-half of its load carrying capacity only. Where, Hydraulic jack was used to apply axial load and it was monitored by the data acquisition and load cell system. Total of four specimens were casted and prepared for testing, including two control specimens, which were tested beyond its ultimate failure strength and remaining two were tested by applying seventy percentage of their ultimate load. After testing, the failed control specimens were repaired by fill the crack portions with cement paste after cleaning the surfaces of sample by sand paper. Same grade of concrete was used in damaged portion and compact it well. The rehabilitated specimens' were placed in fresh water for 28 days of curing and after curing samples wrapped with AFRP sheet in different layers. Remaining two specimens were also wrapped by using aramid fibre.

8.6 RETROFITTING AND STRENGTHEN OF JOINT

The strengthening and retrofitting of beam-column joint take place using AFRP (Aramid Fiber Reinforced Polymer). The beginning step of strengthening and retrofitting the beam-column joint is to repair and close the gap of cracks by injecting hybrid composite made from cement paste and hardener chemical named as Halifix, with hand pressure pump as shown in figure 8.15. It is to ensure that cracks should be perfectly repaired prior to retesting of specimen under monotonic or cyclic load and diagonal cracks at top area of the column were repaired with epoxy coating to cover up structural cracks. The wrapping of AFRP sheets on prime coat epoxy resin (Araldite GY 257 and Hardener HY 840) takes place once the epoxy injection grouting dried as shown in figure 8.16. The column is retrofitted with wrapping three different layers of AFRP sheets from all sides of it and the transverse beam near the joint region was also retrofitted by wrapping three different layers of AFRP sheets on both side of the joint as shown in figure 8.17. After the cracks were treated, specimens kept for required period of curing so that FRP could be set properly and made a perfect bond with concrete.

8.7 BONDING PROCEDURE

Before wrapping the AFRP sheets, the surface and edges of the specimens were ground by mechanical means and surface of concrete was slightly chiselled off with pointed chisel to remove the surface material for enhancing good bonding and cleaned with fresh water to abolish all dirt and debris, and sand paper is used to clean the surface of joint after water wash to make it rough so that AFRP sheet could made better bond with it through epoxy resin. Once the surface of specimen had been prepared, the epoxy resin was prepared. Epoxy resin is the composite of binder and hardener which mixed together in required proportion. Mixing was carried out in the proportion of 1:0.5 with Araldite GY 257 and Hardener HY 840. The epoxy coating was enforced on the specimen and the 1st layer of AFRP sheets was placed over the surface of beam-column joint as shown in 8.17. A hand roller was also used to roll over the surface gently to abolish the voids. After 7 days of curing period, the epoxy coating was enforced over the sheet and then, the second layer of fibre sheet was placed, similarly third layer of sheet was applied. After this complete process of wrapping AFRP sheet with epoxy resin on joint surface and curing time, rehabilitated specimen was prepared for test again as shown in figure 8.18.

Fig 8.11 Compressive Strength Testing Machine

Fig 8.12 Flexural Strength Testing Machine by Centre Point Loading System

Fig 8.13 Split Tensile Strength Test

Fig 8.14 Testing of Beam-Column Joint by Universal Testing Machine

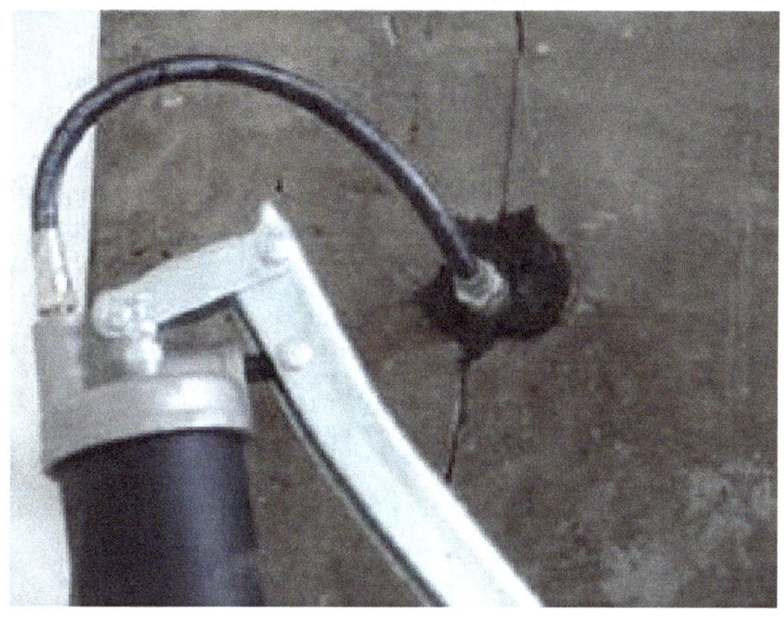

Fig 8.15 Crack Filling by Injecting Method through Hand Pressure Pump

Fig 8.16 Repaired Specimens kept for Sear

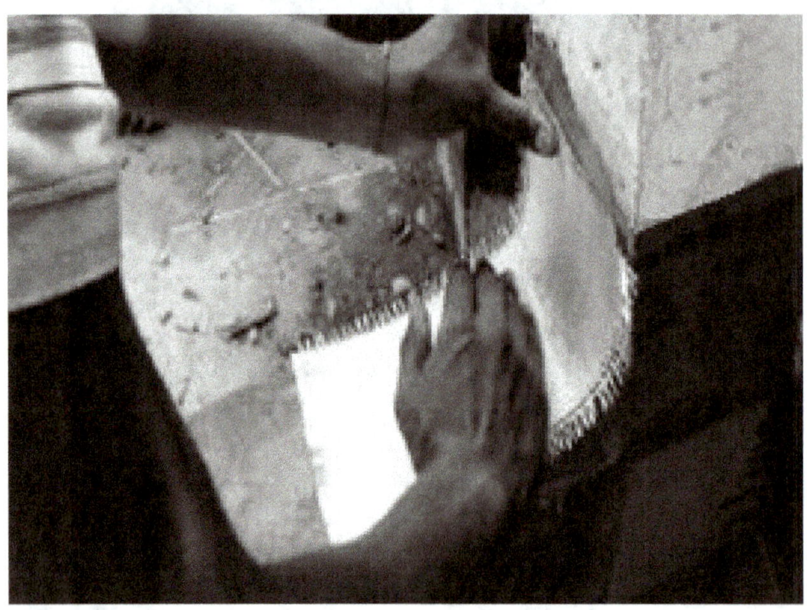

Fig 8.17 Wrapping First Layer of AFRP Sheet over Epoxy Resin

Fig 8.18 Rehabilitate Specimen Prepared for Testing

9

DISCUSSION ON RESULTS

9.1 GENERAL

Behaviour of the tested specimen as well as rehabilitated specimens is discussed in this chapter. The performance of the specimens such as cubes, prisms, cylindrical specimens and exterior beam-column joint specimens with or without AFRP sheet, and also rehabilitated specimens under axial load, cyclic load or monotonic load, are presented. Different specimen's properties of control and retrofitted specimens were compared with each other and after that rehabilitate specimen's properties compared with control and retrofit samples. This chapter shows results on mechanical properties of concrete samples with or without AFRP such as compressive strength of cubical specimens, flexural strength of prism type specimens and split tensile strength of cylindrical shaped specimens, and compared control specimens with AFRP sheet wrapped specimens which are two types retrofitted and rehabilitated. Many of the other properties such as maximum displacement, stiffness, deflection-ductility ratio, yield strength etc of exterior beam-column joint or T-joint under monotonic loading or cyclic loading with or without AFRP, are also discussed in this chapter.

9.2 DISCUSSION ON MECHANICAL PROPERTIES

From the light of the experimental investigation work, behaviour of different specimens found for control and retrofitted system under monotonic loading action with proper required period of curing as per Indian Standards guidelines, going to discuss where compressive strength test, flexural strength test and split tensile strength were conducted on cubical samples, prisms and cylindrical samples, respectively after 1-day, 7-days and 28-days of testing which are given next.

9.2.1 COMPRESSIVE STRENGTH

Compressive strength of cubical samples after required period of wet curing when compared control with AFRP specimens it proposed that there is some increment in compressive strength which is more than 2% of retrofitted specimens as shown in figure 9.1 when it compared with control specimens. This test conducted on 2000kN capacity of compression testing machine under compression axial load as per IS 516:1959 as shown in figure 8.10, and corresponding values of compressive strength results are given in table 9.1. The results came from compression test are in form of maximum load carried by cubical sample before it fail.

The compressive stress or strength (N/mm^2) can be determined by dividing the maximum load carried by cubical samples to its cross-sectional area.

Therefore,

$$\sigma = \frac{P}{A} \, \text{N/mm}^2$$

Where,

P   = Maximum load carried by cubical sample before failure,

A   =Cross-sectional area cube which is nothing but 100mm x 100mm

     =10000 mm^2,

σ =Maximum Compressive Stress (N/mm^2)

The experimental findings which proposed by compressive strength test are in form of maximum load carried by cubical sample before it fail and results showing 2% of increment in load carrying capacity of AFRP samples as compared to control but as all know concrete is strong in compression so this type of fibre reinforced polymer may or may not be used to improve only this mechanical property of concrete.

9.2.2 FLEXURAL STRENGTH

Flexural strength of prisms or beams after required period of wet curing when compared control with AFRP samples it proposed that there is excellent increment in flexural strength or tensile strength which is more than 24% of retrofitted specimens as shown in figure 9.2 when it compared with control specimens. This test conducted on 2000kN capacity of flexural strength testing machine under centre point loading system as per Indian Standard guidelines as shown in figure 8.11, and corresponding values of flexural strength results are given in table 9.2. The corresponding result values found by flexural strength test are in form of maximum load carried by beam under centre-point loading before it fail under bending compression.

The fundamental bending equation which given below, bending stresses can be determined by using it, as shown below:

know that,

$$\frac{M}{I} = \frac{\sigma b}{y}$$

Or can be written as in N/mm^2

$$\sigma b = M \times \frac{I}{y}$$

Where,

M   =Moment of Resistance which is nothing but load in to perpendicular distance (Nmm),

I   =Moment of Inertia about neutral axis which is $\frac{bd^3}{12}$ (mm^4),

σ_b =Bending Stress (N/mm^2),

y   =Extreme fibre distance from neutral axis which is nothing but $\frac{d}{2}$,

b   = Width of Beam (mm), d = Depth of Beam (mm).

The experimental findings which proposed by flexural strength test are in form of maximum load carried by beam under centre-point loading before it fail under bending compression and results showing 24% of increment in load carrying capacity of AFRP samples as compared to control, and as all know concrete is weak in tension and reinforcement is used to make it strong so as per this, aramid fibre reinforced polymer is too useful for concrete to make it strong in tension.

9.2.3 SPLIT TENSILE STRENGTH

Tensile strength on cylindrical samples after required period of wet curing when compared control with AFRP samples found samples it proposed that there is great increment in split tensile strength which is more than 5% of retrofitted specimens as shown in figure 9.3 when it compared with control specimens. This test conducted on 2000kN capacity of compression strength testing machine under transverse loading system on cylindrical specimens as per Indian Standard guidelines as shown in figure 8.12, and corresponding values of split tensile strength results are given in table 9.3. The corresponding result values found by split tensile strength test are in form of maximum load carried by cylindrical samples before it failed.

Table 9.1 Compressive Strength Results

S. No.	Mix	Testing Period	Density of concrete (kg/m^3)	Avg. Compressive Stress (N/mm^2)
1.	Control	1-Day	2473	17.53
		7-Days	2505	33.00
		28-Days	2413	43.89
2.	AFRP	1-Day	2458	24.13
		7-Days	2590	36.33
		28-Days	2520	44.76

The fundamental bending equation which given below, split tensile stresses can be determined by using it, as shown below:

Split Tensile Stresses $= \dfrac{2\,P}{\pi\,D\,L}$

Where,

P = Maximum load carried by cylindrical sample before failure,

D = Diameter of Sample in (mm),

L = Length of sample in (mm).

Table 9.2 Flexural Strength Results

S. No.	Mix	Testing Period	Density of Concrete (kg/m^3)	Avg. Bending Stress (N/mm^2)
1.	Control	7-Days	2467	4.957
		28-Days	2380	6.473
2.	AFRP	7-Days	2453	6.244
		28-Days	2520	8.060

Table 9.3 Split Tensile Strength Results

S. No.	Mix	Testing Period	Density of Concrete (kg/m^3)	Avg. Split Tensile Stress (N/mm^2)
1.	Control	7-Days	2390	3.0
		28-Days	2475	3.89
2.	AFRP	7-Days	2490	3.36
		28-Days	2520	4.10

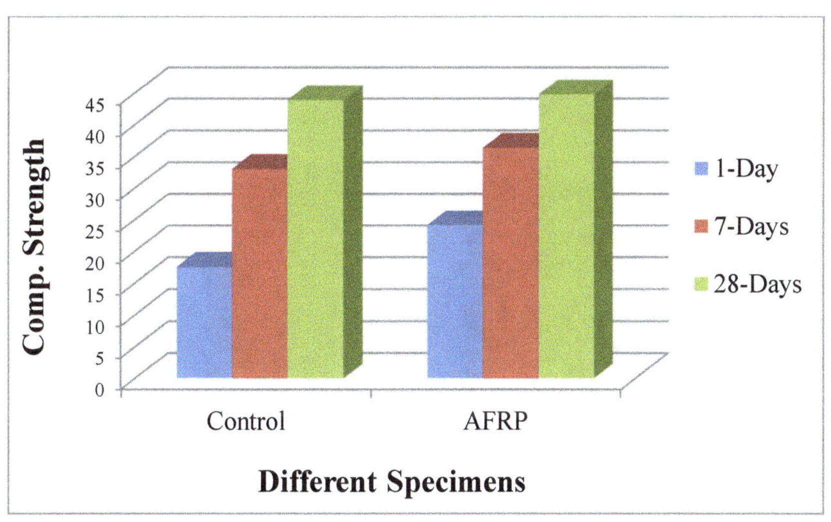

Fig 9.1 Compressive Strength of Specimens

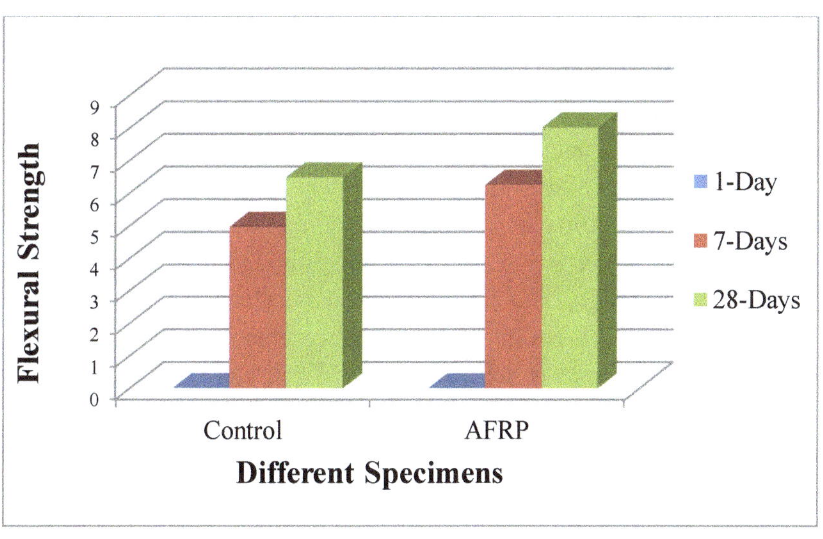

Fig 9.2 Flexural Strength of Specimens

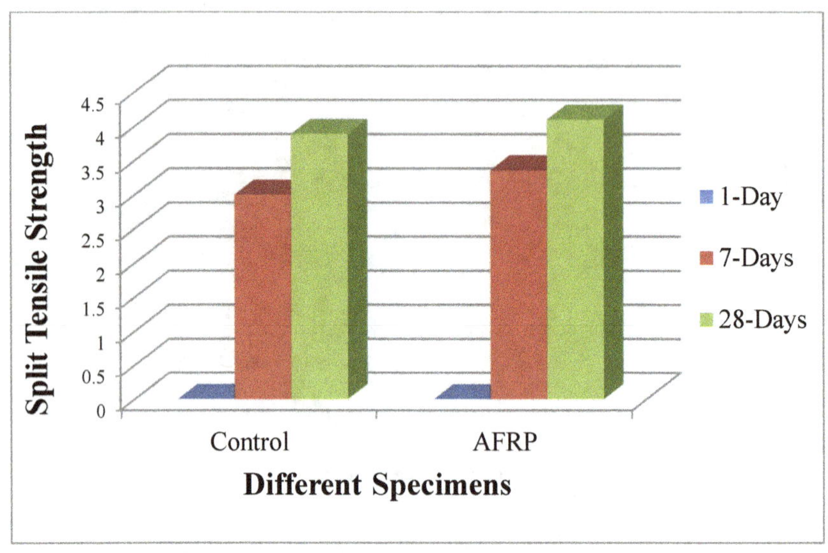

Fig 9.3 Split Tensile Strength of Specimens

9.3 DISCUSSION ON BEAM-COLUMN JOINT PROPERTIES

9.3.1 DESCRIPTION OF RESULTS

Exterior Beam-Column joint is tested under monotonic loading on universal testing machine where found many attributes and behaviour of joint such as maximum deflection under maximum ultimate load, stiffness effect, ductility behaviour from deflection-ductility ratio etc as shown in table 9.4 & 9.5. Stiffness of rehabilitated exterior joint, when compared with control it found 35% increment and when it compared with AFRP specimen results, found that decrement of 36%. Deflection of rehabilitated sample is decreases as 15% and increases as 18% when it compared with control and AFRP specimens, respectively as shown in figure 9.5. Deflection-ductility ratio showing that the ductility of rehabilitated sample is also increases when it compared with control specimens as shown in figure 9.6.

As discussed earlier, testing on beam-column joint conducted on universal testing machine under monotonic loading, by which a new relation of beam column strength is found which is failure comes on column first in control testing but in AFRP sample failure comes first on beam so this is a important result of this test 'strong column weak beam', it will help to prevent fall down the whole structure. Many parameters were found as given in table 9.4 and 9.5, such as stiffness which is nothing but ratio of ultimate load to the maximum displacement, measured in kN/mm and similar results where it increased by more than 35%, are shown in table 9.7 and AFRP sheet helped to reduce deflection of member.

The experimental findings which proposed by exterior beam-column joint or T-shaped joint test are in form of maximum load carried by joint under before it fail under axial gravity load as well as lateral horizontal load on vertex of column and corresponding results showing excellent increment in load carrying capacity of both retrofit and rehabilitate samples by using AFRP sheet as compared to control, great increment in stiffness as well as ductility of joint, and decrement in deflection, make joint strong in both type of loading. At the end of detailed investigation, can say AFRP sheet is a great construction material to make concrete strong and it can be used in retrofitting or rehabilitation work to make stronger the weak joints of structure.

Table 9.4 Values of Initial and Ultimate Cracking Load for Different Specimens

Specimens Type	Specimen Detail	Initial Cracking Load (kN)	Max. Ultimate Load (MUL) (kN)	Yield Load (kN)
Control	C1	5.5	10.5	5.0
	C2	6.0	11.0	5.2
AFRP	A1	7.5	14.5	6.8
	A2	7.0	13.5	6.2
Rehabilitated	R1	6.4	12.0	5.7
	R2	6.2	12.6	5.4

Table 9.5 Values of Deflection-Ductility Ratios and Stiffness

Specimen Types	Specimen Details	Deflection (mm)	Deflection-Ductility Ratios	Stiffness (kN/mm)
Control	C1	11.0	2.20	0.950
	C2	13.5	2.59	0.810
AFRP	A1	8.0	1.17	1.820
	A2	9.5	1.53	1.421
Rehabilitated	R1	10.1	1.77	1.188
	R2	10.6	1.96	1.200

Fig 9.4 Initial & Maximum Ultimate Load of Specimens

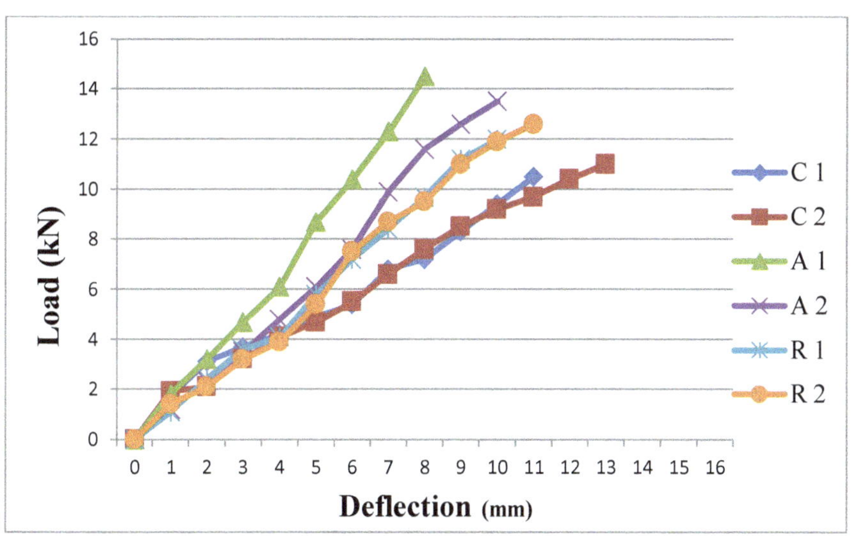

Fig 9.5 Relation of Maximum Ultimate Load & Maximum Deflection or Displacement

Where,

C1 and C2, A1 and A2, and R1 and R2 are the different specimens such as Control 1 and 2, AFRP Specimens 1 and 2, and Rehabilitated Specimens R1 and R2, respectively.

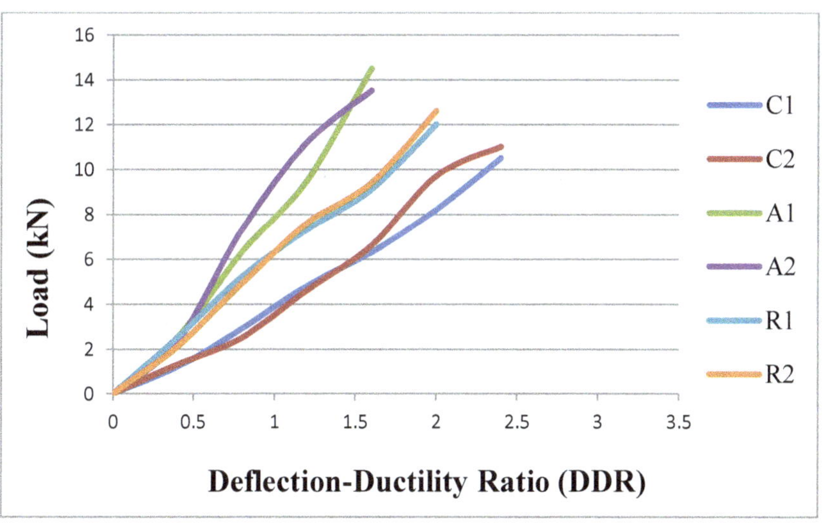

Fig 9.6 Relation of Maximum Ultimate Load & Deflection-Ductility Ratio

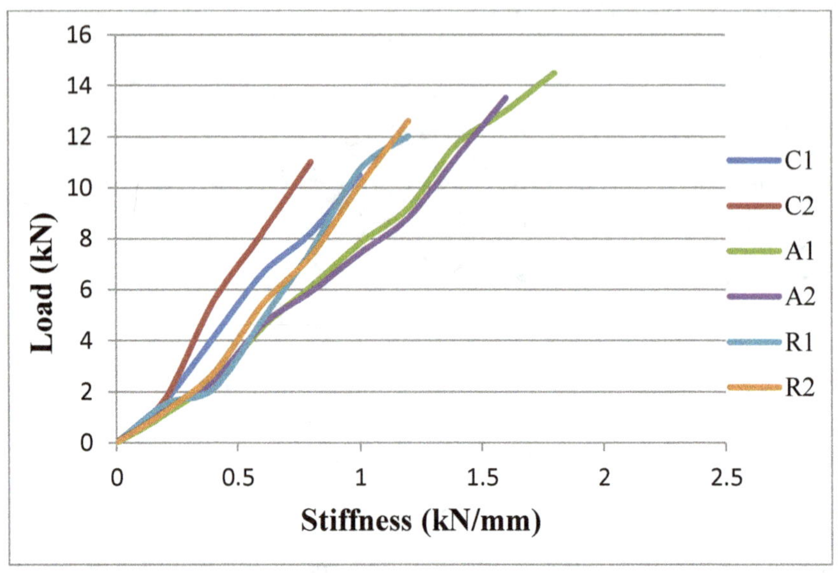

Fig 9.7 Relation of Maximum Ultimate Load & Stiffness

9.4 CONCLUSIONS AND RECOMMENDATIONS

9.4.1 CONCLUSIONS

Based on experimental investigation the following conclusions can be drawn;

a) Mechanical properties such as compressive strength, flexural strength and tensile strength were also found better with AFRP sheet when it compared with control by 2%, 24% and 5% respectively.

b) The above experimentally findings showing, AFRP found to be more efficient for the treatment of exterior beam-column joint. By retrofitting the joint with AFRP sheet, the lateral strength is increased by 14% and the initial cracking strength was found to be increased by 9% when it compared with control specimens.

c) The stiffness of joint also increases by more than 35% and found decrement in maximum deflection value by 15% after rehabilitating when it compared with control specimen results.

d) This type of fibrous material can be beneficial for concrete to convert it brittle to ductile manner as shown in figure 9.6 of deflection-ductility ratio. This unique property conversion is found by compare the deflection-ductility ratio of control and AFRP specimens.

e) In the control specimen, the failure comes in the column but in the retrofitted specimen failure comes in the beam so from this, the strong column weak beam concept is achieved and it helps to prevent the failure of entire structure.

However, after this detailed investigation on behaviour of strengthened exterior beam-column joint and some other specimens for examine the mechanical properties, it concluded that aramid fibre reinforcement polymer (AFRP) sheet is excellent construction material to make concrete stronger in flexural or flexural strength and AFRP sheet is also be useful for retrofit or rehabilitate the structural component to make stronger structure. This study will be helpful to retrofit and rehabilitate that structures which are designed non-seismically or can't be resist earthquake forces and that which needs rehabilitation. AFRP composite provide ductility and stiffness to structure by which structure can resist unwanted forces.

9.4.2 RECOMMENDATIONS FOR FUTURE RESEARCH

The use of FRP in strengthens defected or inferior RC beam-column joint is enhancing in popularity. So far design guidelines and provisions are still not refined enough to applicable in real world of construction. The present experimental study focused on similitude the performance of FRP rehabilitated specimens and deficient or defected specimens. Further studies in same direction should be needed to improve the understanding and performance of fundamental behaviour of FRP-strengthened joints and to refine the numerical or real models in simulating the behaviour of FRP concrete. In general, there is a need of further research efforts which should be devoted to address different problems before the use of FRP in structural applications.

REFERENCES

Journals --

1. Akguzel U. and Pampanin S. (2012) Assessment and Design of Seismic Retrofitting of RC Beam-Column Joints using FRP Composite," Journal of Composites for Construction, 16 (1), p.21-34.

2. Alcocer and Jirsa (1993), "Strengthen the RC Frame Connections Rehabilitated by Jacketing", ACI Structural Journal, V. 90, No. 3, May-June, pp. 249-261.

3. Antonopoulos and Triantafillou T.C. (2002), "Analysis of FRP rehabilitated RC Beam-Column Joints", Journal of Composites for Construction, V. 6, No. 1, February.

4. Antonopoulos and Triantafillo (2003), "Experimental examine the FRP-Strengthened RC Beam-Column Joints", Journal of Composites for Construction, V. 7, No. 1, February.

5. Ayala and Valentini (2003), "Use of FRP Fabric for Strengthening of Reinforced Concrete Beam-Column Joints," Proceedings of Structural Faults plus Repair, The Commonwealth Institute, London, CD-ROM.

6. Balsamo, Colombo and Manfredi (2005), "Seismic Behaviour of a Full-scale RC Frame Repaired by using CFRP Laminates", Engineering Structures, V. 27, pp. 769-780.

7. Beres and Gergely (1992), "Experimental findings of Repaired and Retrofitted Beam-Column Joint", Technical Report NCEER-92-0025, SUNY/Buffalo.

8. Bizindavyi and Erki (2003), "Experimental Investigation of Bonded FRP Concrete Joints under Cyclic Loading", Journal of Composites for Construction, V. 7, No. 2, May.

9. Deniaud and Cheng (2003), "Reinforced Concrete T-Beams Strengthened Fibre Reinforced Polymer Sheets in shear", Journal of Composite for Construction, V. 7, No. 4, November.

10. El-Amoury and Ghobarah (2002), "Seismic Rehabilitation of Beam-Column Joint using GFRP Sheets", Engineering Structures, V. 24, pp. 1397-1407.

11. Engindeniz Kahn and Zureick (2005), "Repair and strengthening of reinforced concrete beam-column joints: state of the art", ACI Structural Journal, V. 102, No. 2, March-April, pp. 187-197.

12. Engindeniz (2008), "Repair and Strengthening of Pre-1970 RC Corner Beam- Column Joints using CFRP Composites," Ph.D. thesis, Georgia Institute of Technology.

13. Filiatrault and Lebrun (2006), "Seismic Rehabilitation of Reinforced Concrete Joints by Epoxy Pressure Injection Technique", Seismic Rehabilitation of Concrete Structures, SP-160, American Concrete Institute, Farmington Hills, Michigan, pp. 73-92.

14. Fujii and Morita (2005), "Comparison between Behaviour of Exterior and Interior Reinforced Beam-Column Joint," ACI-SP 123, Design of Beam-Column Joints for Seismic Resistance, pp. 145-165.

15. Ghobarah and Said (2002), "Shear Strengthening of Beam-Column Joints", Engineering Structures, V. 24, 2002, pp. 881-888.

16. Granata and Parvin (2001), "An Experimental Study on Kevlar Strengthening of Beam-Column Connections", Composite Structures, V. 53, pp. 163-171.

17. Huang K. (2003), "Design of Diagonally Reinforced Interior Beam-Column Joints for Moderately Seismicity Regions", Ph.D. Thesis, The University of Hong Kong.

18. Hakuto, Park and Tanaka (2000), "Seismic Load Tests on Interior and Exterior Beam-Column Joints with Substandard Reinforcing Details," ACI Structure Journal, 97(1), 11-25.

19. Hamid and Ghani (2013)," Retrofitting of Beam-Column Joint Using CFRP and Steel Plate", International Journal of Civil, Environmental, Structural, Construction and Architectural Engineering Vol:7, No:12, 2013.

20. Kay and Hamid (2012), Seismic Performance of SFRC Beam-Column Joint with Corbel Under Reversible Lateral Cyclic Loading, IACSIT International Journal of Engineering and Technology, ISSN 1793-8236, Vol.4, No.1, February 2012,p.76-80.

21. Kim and LaFave (2007), "Key Influence Parameters for the Joint Shear Behavior of Reinforced Concrete (RC) Beam-Column Connections," Engineering Structures, 29, pp. 2523-2539.

22. Lakshmi and Dutta (2008), "Numerical Study of Strengthening of Beam-Column Joints under Cyclic Excitation Using FRP Composites," Journal of Structural Engineering, 35, pp. 59-65.

23. Lowes and Altoontash (2003), "Modeling Reinforced-Concrete Beam- Column Joints Subjected to Cyclic Loading," ACSE Journal of Structural Engineering, 129(12), pp. 1686-1697.

24. Mahini and Ronagh (2004), "CFRP-retrofitted RC Exterior Beam Column Connections under Cyclic Loads," FRP Composites in Civil Engineering, 31, 647-652.

25. Menon, Sarkar and Agrawal (2007), "Design of RC Beam-Column Joints under Seismic Loading - A Review," Journal of Structural Engineering, 33, pp. 449 457.

26. Mukherjee A. and Joshi M. (2005), "FRPC Reinforced Concrete Beam-Column Joints under Cyclic Excitation", Composite Structures, 70, pp. 185-199.

27. Nehdi and Said (2005), "Behavior of Hybrid (Steel-GFRP) Reinforced Concrete Frames under Reversed Cyclic Loading," Materials and Structures, 38(280), pp. 627-637.

28. Ramakrishna and Ravindra (2012)," Experimental Investigation on Rehabilitation of Reinforced Cement Concrete Interior Beam-Column Joints using CFRP and GFRP Sheets", International Journal of Engineering Science and Technology, Vol. 4 No.03 March 2012.

29. Said and Nehdi (2004), "Use of FRP for RC Frames in Seismic Zones: Part I. Evaluation of FRP Beam-Column Joint Rehabilitation Techniques", Applied Composite Materials, V. 11, pp. 205-226.

30. Shannag and Dyya (2005), "Lateral Load Response of High Performance Fibre Reinforced Concrete Beam-Column Joints," Journal of Construction and Building Materials, 19, pp. 500-508.

31. Subramanian and Rao, "Seismic Design of Joints in RC Strucutres, The Indian Concrete Journal, February 2003, Vol.77, No.2, pp. 883-892.

32. Tsonos (2008), "Effectiveness of CFRP Jackets and RC Jackets In Post Earthquake and Pre Earthquake Retrofitting of Beam Column Sub-Assemblages," Journal of Engineering Structures, 30, pp. 777-793.

Books –

1. Neelam Sharma (2012), "R.C.C. Design and Drawing", S.K. Kataria and Sons Publisher, New Delhi, chapter No. 5,6,8,11, third revised edition.

2. R.S. Khurmi and N. Khurmi (2014), "Strength of Materials", S. Chand and Company Publisher, New Delhi, chapter No. 2,11,12,13,16,19,34, fifteenth edition.

3. S K Duggal (2012), "limit State Design of Structures." Tata McGraw Hill publisher, New Delhi, tenth edition.

4. A.M. Neville (2010)," Concrete technology," Longman group Publisher, United Kingdom, Second edition.

5. Krishan Kumar (2002), "Repair and Rehabilitation of RCC Buildings," Director General Works, Central Public Works Department, Govt of India, New Delhi, First Edition.

6. Paz and Leigh (2004), "Structural Dynamics: Theory and Computation," Kluwer Academic Publisher Group, Netherlands, Fifth edition.

7. Murty, Goswami and Mehta (2004), "Earthquake Behaviour of Buildings," GSDMA Publication, first Edition.

Indian Standard Codes –

1. IS Code 13920:1993, "Ductile Detailing of Reinforced Concrete Structures Subjected to Seismic Forces".

2. IS Code 1893:2002, "Criteria for Earthquake Resistant Design of Structures".

3. IS Code 456:2000, "For Plain and Reinforced Concrete".